D1211749

grow your own
cut flowers

BBC

grow your own
cut flowers

photographs by jonathan buckley

WINDING
STAIR
PRESS

To Adam, Rosie and Molly

Grow Your Own Cut Flowers
Original edition text copyright © 2002 by Sarah Raven
North American edition © 2002 by Winding Stair Press
Photographs copyright © Jonathan Buckley 2002
First Published by **BBC Worldwide Limited,** Woodlands, 80 Wood
Lane, London W12 0TT
The moral rights of the author have been asserted

All rights reserved. The use of any part of this publication reproduced,
transmitted in any form or by any means, electronic, mechanical,
photocopying, recording or otherwise, or stored in a retrieval system,
without prior written consent of the publisher is an infringement of
 the copyright law. In the case of photocopying or other reprographic
copying, a license from the Canadian Copyright Licensing Agency
(CANCOPY) may be obtained.

National Library of Canada Cataloguing in Publication Data

Raven, Sarah
   Grow your own cut flowers

North American ed.
Includes index.
ISBN 1-55366-265-2

1. Flower gardening. 2. Cat flowers. 3. Flower arrangement.
I. Title.

SB405.R39 2002   635.9'66   2002-900543-4

Winding Stair Press
An imprint of Stewart House Publishing Inc.
290 North Queen Street, #210
Etobicoke, Ontario, M9C 5K4
Canada
1-866-574-6873
www.stewarthouse.com

Executive Vice President and Publisher: Ken Proctor
Director of Publishing and Product Acquisition: Joe March
Production Manager: Ruth Bradley-St-Cyr
North Americanization: Rebecka Sheffield and Laura Brady
Commissioning Editor Vivien Bowler
Copy Editor Lin Hawthorne
Project Editor Vicki Vrint
Art Direction Pene Parker and Lisa Pettibone
Design Andrew Barron @ Thextension

This book is available at special discounts for bulk purchases by
groups or organizations for sales promotions, premiums, fundraising
and educational purposes. For details, contact: Stewart House
Publishing Inc., Special Sales Department, 195 Allstate Parkway,
Markham, Ontario L3R 4T8. Toll free 1-866-474-3478.

1 2 3 4 5 6   07 06 05 04 03 02

contents

Introduction

Please give up the idea that by picking flowers you're somehow depleting the beauty of what you have outside your window. The very opposite is the case. In fact, that's what this book is about. If you grow the right plants, picking their buds and blooms will ensure the garden will go on looking fuller and brighter for longer. You can fill your house with flowers, have enough to take bunches to friends, and have a garden that will still look superb for most of the year. A phrase I've known since I was a child, 'It's the generous gardener who has the most flowers', remains a governing principle for me.

Most of us have predominantly shrub and perennial plants in our borders. Why not make room for a small patch, or several scattered areas, and fill them with cut-and-come-again flowers? These are plants that quickly re-grow after picking – there will be more flowers to pick within a couple of days. This generous characteristic applies to all hardy and half-hardy annuals, most biennials, and all dahlias, like this one, right, 'Rip City'.

If you are already half-converted and use bedding annuals and biennials in patches between your perennials and shrubs to add more interest to your garden, why not replace these with different varieties, in clear, single colors, with tall, straight stems, rather than the usual, mixed-color, pigmy forms? You'll have as much color as before – if not more – and with these, you'll have flowers ideal for picking and arranging. They can decorate your house as well as your garden.

Supplement what they provide with some spring and summer flowering bulbs – tulips, hyacinths, alliums and lilies – and you'll have flower arrangements for the picking from March until November, and they're right there, within a minute of your kitchen table.

You don't need huge amounts of space; in fact, you can grow your own cut flowers in pots on a windowsill. You don't need a big budget; all these plants are cheap and easy to grow. All you need is some packets of seed, and a few bulbs and tubers. You don't even need as much time as you would imagine. A patch of twelve square metres, say 3 x 4m (9 x 12ft), will give you enough flowers easily, and all it needs is an average of two hours' work a week in the busiest months – March until October. This is adaptable. If you don't have that much time, make the patch smaller. You'll just have slightly fewer flowers. At the other extreme, if you want to grow enough flowers to sell, increase the area for planting. Whether it's a large or a small patch, you don't need to have gardened before. There is everything here to get you going. All gardening instructions are described in a simple, recipe-style form and there are some easy tips to help you make some wonderful, life-enhancing arrangements. You'll find a key to the flowers used in each arrangement at the end of the book (see page 144).

cut-and-come-again flowers

The term is self-explanatory: you pick them and, within days, the flowers have come again. To get bucketsful of cut flowers from a small plot of ground, you need to devote most of the soil to growing cut-and-come-again flowering plants.

Creating a cutting patch

I use three groups of cut-and-come-again flowers: they are all 'king' producers – plants that will go on to produce buckets of flowers for several months at a stretch. Annuals, such as sunflowers, sweet peas, scabious and snapdragons; biennials, such as sweet Williams and Iceland poppies; and rich, intensely colored dahlias.

With the cut-and-come-again club, the more you pick, the more they flower – the perfect qualification for a cutting-patch plant. If you fill your beds with shrubs and perennials, your cut-flower crop will be limited. Once you've picked stems of delphiniums, phlox and agapanthus, spectacular as they are, that's it – there won't be any more and your garden and the view will have suffered from your harvest. It's true that if you grow the right delphiniums and feed them well after their summer flowering, you may get a second, lesser flush of flowers in the early autumn, but, as far as cutting goes, the yield is still relatively small.

How it works

The cut-and-come-agains only stop producing when they run to seed, or when they get tired at the end of their season. If you grow sweet peas, winter-flowering pansies, or petunias, you'll probably already know that you must constantly pick, or dead-head, for the flowers to keep going. The same is true of all annuals and dahlias and of most biennials.

But rather than dead-heading, why not pick earlier and choose live-heading? By that I mean picking the buds and flowers when they are in their prime, to bring them into the house, rather than removing them as they brown and die. It makes no difference to the plant and won't deplete or exhaust it. In fact, the opposite is true; picking encourages the plant to produce more flowers. The flowers are there to reproduce and their aim is to make as many seeds as possible. If you steal the flowers – the means of reproduction – the plants have to go on and make more. You pick, they produce, you pick, they produce. It's an ever-filling cup.

Prime producers

Compare a square plot planted with peonies with one stocked with cutting annuals. From the peonies, you'll pick one or two buckets of blooms over a period of about two to three weeks. From the same space given over to English or pot marigolds (*Calendula officinalis*) or honeywort (*Cerinthe major* 'Purpurascens') you can pick a bucket of flowers twice a week for two months – and the plants will still be flowering. With half-hardy annuals, such as snapdragons, nicotianas, rudbeckias and cosmos, all famed for their length of flowering, the picking season will be twice as long – four or five months, not just two. Of course, you have to sow annuals every year, but it seems to me it's a classic case of only getting out what you put in.

What's more, unless they're very cleverly designed, purely perennial borders can be brown and colorless in the autumn. June and July are their peak months, and by August, most perennials will almost certainly have done their stuff. Not so with annuals and dahlias. If you keep picking, your garden will be full to the brim until late autumn.

Low costs, high returns

Hardy annuals are the cheapest plants you can grow. They need no special kit, apart from a rake and perhaps a hoe. Because you don't need to buy expensive plants, you can chuck them out if you don't like the color. You can experiment and be brave. If you get it wrong with a few of the annuals, or dahlias – a couple of next-door colors jar, or you don't like the shape and texture of one of your attempts – rip them out and start again. It hasn't cost much and you can have another go straight away, or wait until next year. It's ideal gardening for a learner. You lose little – but gain a lot of knowledge – by making mistakes.

Annuals, biennials and dahlias are unfussy and easy to grow. They thrive on most soils in full sun and are ideal whether you're an expert gardener, or have never picked up a spade before. They are vigorous, quick-

(Below) My cutting garden has four central beds which are filled with annuals and biennials. As soon as a line **stops producing lots of flowers, it is taken out and replaced with something with a later flowering season.** **All four beds are edged with *Euphorbia oblongata*: it is the best foliage plant and the greatest producer of the lot.**

growing plants, with few pest and disease problems – perfect for the organic gardener. Dahlias do need to be watered and fed well and you need to scatter earwig traps in amongst the plants (see page 117), but you certainly don't need to spray. All flowers for cutting need to be staked, but that's as far as it goes. Compare this to the fuss involved in growing perfect picking roses. If you grow the right repeat-flowering forms, they have a picking season of several months and they smell and look lovely, but they need too much attention for me. To get perfect, flawless foliage and flowers that will look good in the house, you'll be feeding and watering them regularly. You'll probably also have to spray twice a month with an insecticide and fungicide, which I really would rather not do.

I love the immediacy, cheapness and flexibility of growing annuals and biennials from seed. Dahlias from tubers and rooted stem cuttings are just as easy. To fill a patch doesn't break the bank and the plants romp

away, growing 30cm (12in) a week if the weather's right. You'll be cutting flowers three months after sowing or planting. This is instant beauty, easily achieved. With perennials, roses and shrubs, you'll have to wait two or three years before a decent harvest and, unless you build it up gradually by propagating everything yourself, the outlay is huge in comparison. And you're stuck with the colors and plants you choose.

There's just one important thing to remember. When picking the cut-and-come-agains, don't cut the flowering stem to the ground. Leave a few side branches, or axillary buds (a bud between the stem and leaf) below your cut. These will go on to be next week's flower (see page 130).

And for the perfect cut-flower plot, don't forget bulbs. They may be more expensive and are not cut-and-come-again, but they give the place real glamour. You want a good smattering of tulips, as well as some alliums and lilies, at the very least, to complete the plot.

Plant rotation

For a seamless supply of cut flowers from spring until late autumn, follow this system of plant rotation. You need to remove plants as they get tired to clear some space for a new, more energetic crop. This intensive system uses every bit of soil, every month of the year. There is never a fallow period.

I don't use fertilizers to keep this productivity going. Too much nitrogen encourages the plants to make lots of lush leaves with fewer flowers. Plants like honeywort, California poppies, bupleurum, dill, greater quaking grass and corn poppies all do best in poor, gritty ground. Self-sown on my gravel paths, these plants always thrive and flower well.

Instead of fertilizing, I mulch everything with compost – my own homemade if I have enough, and bought-in mushroom compost when I don't. My homemade compost is made with lots of straw to bulk it out, which stops it becoming too rich. Whenever I plant a new row, it's mulched 5cm (2in) deep, leaving a bare strip, 2.5–5cm (1–2in) across, around the plant's crown (where it meets the soil). The mulch keeps weeds under control. It also helps improve the conditions of heavy clay and light sand and adds just enough fertility to keep the ground producing well. If the mulch hasn't already been drawn into the soil by the earthworms, or rotted down completely, it's incorporated as I dig or rototill before the next lot of plants go in. These are then mulched too.

There are a couple of things to be wary about with mushroom compost. If it's not organic, it can come with chemicals included! If you garden on alkaline soil, mushroom compost is not the organic material for you. It often comes with chalk chips mixed in – a fine addition on acid soils, but it's not a good idea to add in huge bulk if your soil is already limy. Use your own, or municipal green compost (if available, check with your local authority), leaf mold, or composted bark. The last three can be more expensive, but have a near neutral or slightly acid pH.

Ensuring continuity

These are some of the stalwarts that I grow to ensure a continuity of material for arranging through the year. The most important plant is *Euphorbia oblongata*. I pick it from spring until the autumn – it's the best basic foliage plant you can grow. I use it to edge my four central beds.

Spring

Early-flowering hardy annuals: autumn-sown honeywort (*Cerinthe major* 'Purpurascens'), *Euphorbia oblongata*

Early-flowering biennials: wallflowers, *Euphorbia lathyris*, honesty (*Lunaria annua*)

Bulbs: hyacinths, narcissi, fritillaries and tulips

Spring-flowering perennials: euphorbias, hellebores and cardoon (*Cynara cardunculus*) for foliage

Late spring – early summer

Hardy annuals: *Euphorbia oblongata*, marigolds (*Calendula*), cornflowers (*Centaurea cyanus*), California poppies (*Eschscholzia californica*) etc

Sweet peas: all

Biennials: foxgloves (*Digitalis*), *Anchusa*, Iceland poppies

(*Papaver nudicaule*), sweet Williams (*Dianthus barbatus*) etc

Bulbs: alliums and lilies

A few summer-flowering perennials: peonies, lysimachia and white perennial stocks (*Matthiola*)

High summer

Half-hardy annuals: snapdragons (*Antirrhinum*), *Cleome, Cosmos, Rudbeckia, Zinnia* etc

Hardy annuals: *Euphorbia oblongata, Scabiosa*, sunflowers (*Helianthus annuus*), *Atriplex* (for seedheads)

Bulbs: lilies and gladioli

Dahlias: all

Autumn

Half-hardy annuals: *Cleome, Nicotiana, Rudbeckia, Zinnia*

Hardy annuals: *Euphorbia oblongata, Scabiosa atropurpurea* and sunflowers (*Helianthus annuus*)

Dahlias: all

Perennials: *Phlox* and *Helenium*

Shrubs and trees: *Viburnum opulus*, hydrangeas and colorful autumn leaves

What you need to create a cutting patch

As a very rough rule of thumb, you'll need to spend ten minutes a week on each square meter of your cutting patch. If you think that, from March until October, you have two hours a week you can devote to this, then you can cultivate a patch of twelve square meters, say 3 x 4m (9 x 12ft), will give you masses of flowers. It will produce at least two or three bunches of flowers, twice a week in the peak season from mid-April to mid-September, and one bunch twice a week for a month or six weeks before and after that.

Making the most of it

To make the best use of a small area, divide your patch into a central zone (about 70 percent of the ground) with a narrow margin around the outside. In the center, put your annuals and biennials. In the outer circle, put your bulbs, dahlias, perennials and shrubs (see my cutting patch design, pages 16–17). With this plan, your plot, however small, will pump out the flowers for nine months at a stretch.

You may not want – or be able – to create a segregated patch for your cutting flowers. But you can scatter patches amongst established plants in your flowerbeds. If your 3 x 4m (9 x 12ft) patch is spread over four or five areas at the front of your mixed shrub and herbaceous beds, it works equally well. It just takes a little more time to pick and maintain than a single patch.

Even if you don't have a garden, you can grow cut flowers in pots on a balcony or window ledge. Don't go for towering, two-meter stems. Restrict yourself to plants that reach 45–60cm (18–24in) in height and you'll be fine. Snapdragons, *Euphorbia oblongata*, marigolds, cerinthe and *Salvia viridis* are all perfect for pots. You'll need to water and feed more than you would with plants grown in the ground, but don't over-do it. If you use terracotta pots, line them with black plastic to cut down on water evaporation. You don't want to create a pond, so pierce the bottom of the plastic with several holes.

A prime site

Choose a sunny, warm site with shelter from the wind. Don't shove your plot right to the back of the garden in amongst trees. People often worry that a cutting patch, as many vegetable gardens do, will look messy or bare for several months at a time. The reverse is the case: if you keep picking, it will keep flowering. It may well be the best bit of your garden – don't hide it away.

It's worth remembering that shade delays seed germination, and wind and shade decrease plant growth. Try to avoid ground beneath a canopy of trees. The roots of a tree reach as far as the branch canopy and are very demanding of water and nutrients.

Wind will restrict growth of plants and delay their establishment. It will also cause havoc, breaking branches and stems if your plants are not supported. Because of this, if you garden in an exposed site, you must install windbreaks. The ideal windbreak is something that forms a semi-permeable barrier to the wind, breaking its force, but allowing it to filter through, rather than just displacing it up into the air. Hedges are ideal; walls and panel fences are not. Solid barriers deflect wind upwards and create turbulence on the leeward side. Walls do, however, have the advantage of absorbing heat in the day, and continuing to radiate it through the evening and night.

(Below) Windbreaks surround my cutting garden.

(Pages 14–15) Two of my cutting beds in late June.

A plan for a cutting patch

Bed F

Dahlias are individually staked at 3ft intervals. Leave them in the ground after frosts, mulching with a 4in layer of compost or straw. You will only need to remove from the ground if you experience temperatures below 25°F.

Dahlia 'Rip City' x 1
Dahlia 'Autumn Luster' x 1
Dahlia 'Geerlings Jubilee' x 1

Bed E

A dark color mix of sweet peas. Make a sweet pea teepee from hazel pea sticks. They are better than canes because twigs help support the plants as they climb. Take out the plants in July and replace with dahlias, such as 'Rip City' or 'Black Fire', which you have been growing on in 1½ gallon pots.

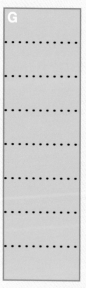

Bed G

Alternate spring bulbs such as tulips in 12in strips, one right next to another. (You don't need a path in between as you can pick them from either side) Dead-head all bulbs as they go over (if you haven't picked them) and mulch with a 2in layer of manure to help promote good flowers next year. (For overplanting, see caption to Bed H.)

Bed A

Net the whole bed to a height of 12in. (If your garden is not sheltered you may need another layer, taking the netting on this bed up to 2½ft.) The plants are in L-shaped rows, 16in apart.

A1 *Amaranthus caudatus* 'Viridis' x 4
A2 *Amaranthus* 'Hopi Red Dye' x 3
A3 *Amaranthus caudatus* 'Viridis' x 3
A4 *Cosmos bipinnatus* 'Purity' x 8
A5 *Tithonia* x 4 and *Cleome* 'Helen Campbell' x 4

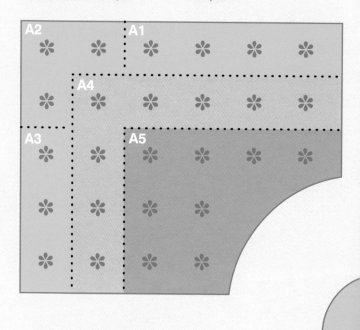

Bed C

Net the bed (apart from the euphorbias) to a height of 12in. The ammi and scabious may need another layer taking the netting up to 2½ft. The plants are in L-shaped rows, 12in apart, except for the euphorbias, and ammi which are 16in apart.

C1 *Antirrhinum* 'Liberty Crimson' x 5
C2 *Scabiosa atropurpurea* x 9
C3 *Ammi majus* x 8
C4 *Euphorbia oblongata* x 10

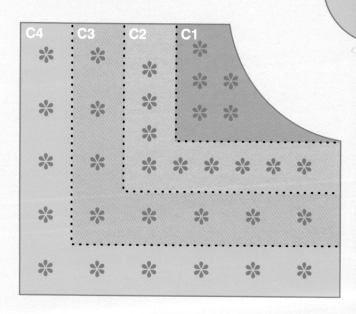

Bed B

Net the whole bed to a height of 12in. The plants are in L-shaped rows, the euphorbias are 16in apart and the others are 12in apart.

B1 *Euphorbia oblongata* x 10
B2 *Nigella hispanica* x 8
B3 *Zinnia* 'Sprite Mix' x 15
B4 *Moluccella laevis* x 10

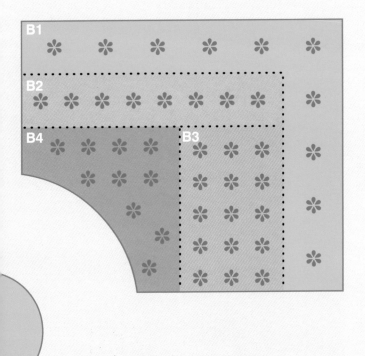

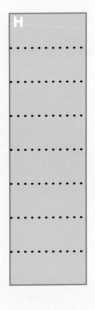

Bed H

(For planting see caption to Bed G.) In late May, when the spring bulbs and tulips are over, you can plant leafy half-hardy vegetables or flowers, such as zucchini, pumpkins, nicotiana or amaranthus. You will not disturb the bulbs as they are deeply planted, but do not cut and clear the bulb foliage until it has browned.

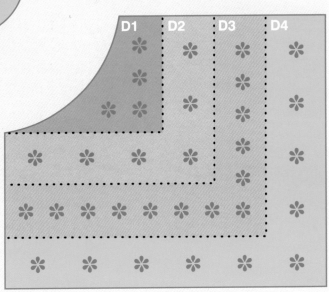

Bed I

Dahlias are individually staked at 3ft intervals. Leave them in the ground after frosts, mulching with a 4in layer of compost or straw. You will only need to remove from the ground if you experience temperatures below 25°F.

Dahlia 'Inglebrook Jill' x 1
Dahlia 'Raffles' x 1
Dahlia 'Black Fire' x 1

This cutting patch is 24 x 33ft. All the paths are 2¹/₂ft. The plot should be situated in a sunny, sheltered place.

It is a large patch. If you don't have this much room, plant bulbs and dahlias somewhere else and get rid of a central row in each section (A, B, C and D), e.g. remove D3 and split D2, growing calendulas in half of it.

Bed D

Net the whole bed to a height of 12in. The malope are 16in apart and the cerinthe, salvia and the calendula are 12in apart. (For instructions on netting see page 51.)

D1 *Salvia viridis* 'Blue' x 4
D2 *Malope trifida* 'Vulcan' x 6
D3 *Calendula officinalis* 'Indian Prince' x 13
D4 *Cerinthe major* 'Purpurascens' x10

17

(Below) These woven hazel
hurdles make wonderful
windbreaks. They look pretty
and are practical too.

(Below right) The rich colors
of the glasses and bowls are
picked up by the flowers –
dahlias, zinnias and tithonia.

They therefore create their own microclimate. When
you're thinking how high to make the shelter, remember
that windbreaks protect over a distance of five times
their height, with some effect over eight times.

It's a good tip, often repeated, to observe the area
you are thinking of using for as long as possible before
you plant. I'm impatient by nature, but it's well worth
delaying your choice until you get a feel for the best
possible place. Make a note of the hours of sunlight,
where it falls, and wind and frost patterns. You want a
prime site, or series of sites, for this intensive garden
and you'll curse yourself if you go to the trouble of
setting it up and it's wrong. I've done that too many
times.

A nearby outside water supply is also a good
idea. You'll need copious amounts of water to settle
plants in, so bear this in mind when siting your patch.

Structure

To make your cutting beds easy to look after, keep
perennials, bulbs and dahlias separate. I plant them
around the outside of my annuals and biennials areas,
so that the central part of the plot can be dug over, or
rototilled, at any time without the worry of disturbing
perennial roots, or digging up tubers and bulbs. It's a
pain digging around and coming up with a handful of
bulbs that need to be replanted with every other spadeful.
I leave my bulbs in the ground, expecting a harvest from
them for several years before they need to be replaced.
Even if you go for a series of scattered plots, to make
maintenance easy, keep this separation in mind.

Paths

You also need more paths than usual. Paths can be
temporary earth or shingle, or permanent brick or
stone. They should be a minimum of 60cm (2ft) wide.
Anything narrower will be obliterated as the plants grow.
If you can afford the space, make the paths wider.
I usually go for a minimum width of 90cm (3ft).

This makes picking much easier when the plants are fully grown. In the plan on the previous page the paths are all 75cm (2½ft) wide.

If you're planting in rows, put a path in every three or four rows, so that you can reach the picking area from all sides. If you can't reach easily to harvest your flowers, you probably won't, and they'll run to seed and stop producing. That's likely to discourage you. Everything has to be easy to get at. If you're planting in hazy-edged blocks, not rows, measure the length of your arm and design the width between paths around this. Make the beds twice the length of your reach and you'll be able to reach to pick from either side without trampling all over the soil.

Choosing the ingredients for an arrangement

Whether I'm making a small vase to go on the kitchen table, or a vast arrangement for the altar in a church, I follow the same basic recipe and I follow it from the moment I go out into the garden to pick the flowers, right through to adding them, one by one, to the vase. Use this recipe and flower arranging becomes easy. For most arrangements, I pick six ingredients – three foliage plants and three flowers. I arrange the foliage first and then I move on to the flowers.

The primary foliage

Foliage needs three characteristics to qualify for this all-important role.

Firstly, it must be interesting – dark, green-leaved laurels or rhododendrons are boring and will not do. They're heavy and over-dominant, and drown out all but the chunkiest of flowers. All these glossy-leaved ever-greens give an old-fashioned feel. An acidic green is, by far, my favorite color for a base. It is a good foil for all colors and I use it in almost every bunch I make. It goes well with calm pastels, adding sharpness. It also works well with bright, rich colors, highlighting their intensity. *Euphorbia oblongata* is my favorite of all.

Secondly, to work well, primary foliage must have a woodiness to the stem – a substantial character that allows it to fulfil the role of scaffolding – a skeleton on which the rest of the bunch hangs. It acts like a sieve. You gather five or seven primary stems together in a vase, or in your hand, and then drop all the other ingredients in around them. Like the metal in a sieve, primary foliage holds each stem firmly in place.

Thirdly, it must have a slender stem, but a full, dome-shaped top, rather than a spike. With only three or five stems in your hand, you have the base of your bunch and you'll have filled hardly any space in the neck of your vase. If you use something with a fat stem and similar diameter top, you'll fill half the neck of the vase with a single ingredient.

Concentrate on growing lots of primaries – you'll need them for most arrangements.

Anchusa	*Amaranthus*
Atriplex hortensis var. *rubra*	*Eryngium planum*
Euphorbia schillingii	*Euphorbia oblongata*
Helleborus corsicus	*Nicotiana tabacum*
Nigella damascena (whole stems)	*Viburnum opulus*

(Opposite) The six different ingredients for a medium-sized vase. From left to right: the primary, secondary and tertiary foliage and flowers – the bride, bridesmaid and gatecrasher. For flower varieties see p144.

The secondary foliage

This is the foliage filler, or flower-foliage filler. It must be interesting, ideally making a contrast in color and shape to your primary. If it looks too similar, you might as well just add more of the first. Secondary foliage needs to fill the gaps in the primary, through the middle and around the edge, filling out the dome. Almost anything will fill this role.

Spring	
honesty (*Lunaria annua*)	honeywort (*Cerinthe*)
wallflowers (*Erysimum cheiri*)	
Summer	
Ammi majus	*Anchusa*
Atriplex	*Bupleurum*
Cerinthe	dill
Euphorbia lathyris	*Nicotiana*
Autumn	
Amaranthus	*Nicotiana*

The tertiary foliage

I want my flower arrangements to look like a piece of the garden. The third foliage plant, which I use as an upper story, is crucial for this. Use something with an interesting silhouette to give the arrangement a three-dimensional horizon, with ups and downs, as you would see in the garden. I'm not keen on neat, flat plateaus of flowers. Using an upper story avoids that.

Spring	
emerging spring leaves	pussy willow
spikes of blossom	
Summer	
grasses	*Lunaria* seedpods
Lysimachia	*Nigella*
poppy seed cases	*Salvia viridis*
Autumn	
Amaranthus	berries or rose hips
Moluccella	*Nicandra physalodes*

The bride

The bride is really the main focus of the bunch – the dominant flower. Add them in uneven numbers, spreading the flowers throughout the bunch.

Cleome hassleriana cultivars	dahlias
gallica roses	Iceland poppies (*Papaver nudicaule*)
lilies	sunflowers (*Helianthus annuus*)
tulips	zinnias

The bridesmaid

This is the sidekick to the bride, with flowers of a similar color, but smaller. This flower will emphasize and back up the bride, but not compete for center stage. If, for example, I am using an orange parrot tulip, or lily-flowered tulip, as the bride, I might add orange calendulas, or the wallflower, *Erysimum cheiri* 'Fireking'; if using crimson-black sweet Williams, I add crimson-black cornflowers; with white Iceland poppies, I would choose white sweet rocket (*Hesperis matronalis*) and with pink dahlias, pink zinnias are perfect.

The gatecrasher or rebel

This is the punchy contrast to make the bunch sing – something that sticks out, even clashes with the rest of the flowers. Without this, the arrangement ends up too polite and boring. With it, the bunch captures your attention and looks complete. I tend to use strong, contrasting colors. Look at the color choices and juxtapositions in the compositions of great paintings, such as those of Howard Hodgkin, Titian, or Matisse. Artists often make great gardeners and flower arrangers because they understand color theory – what goes with what. Try to experiment with the way colors work with each other. For example, if you've used orange flowers, add blue, or even braver, cerise pink; if you've used crimson, add gold; if you've used white, add blue, or bright lime-green; if you've used bright pink, add turquoise; if you've used primrose, add smokey-purple. Take a look at the color combinations on the following page to see what I mean.

Color combinations

(Opposite) top left, pink
Dahlia 'Geerlings Jubilee'
with, top right, turquoise
Salvia patens 'Cambridge
Blue'; bottom left, acid-green
Nicotiana alata 'Lime-green'
with, bottom right, magenta
Malope trifida 'Vulcan'.

(Below) top left, orange zinnia
with, top right, purple
Cerinthe major; bottom left,
gold *Helianthus debilis* 'Pan'
with, bottom right, crimson
Amaranthus 'Intense Purple'.

The essential perennials

I don't use many perennials for picking, but there are a few I would not be without. Some are highly productive, sharing, at least in part, the cut-and-come-again character of annuals while others, like peonies and delphiniums are just so beautiful, I have to grow them.

Cynara cardunculus, Cardoon

1.8m (6ft) or more
Climate zones 7–9

Description
Spectacular silver, arrowhead-shaped leaves, wonderful from the moment they emerge from the soil in late winter. Large, handsome, purple, thistle flowers in mid- to late summer. If you have less room, choose the smaller member of the same family, *Cynara scolymus* (artichoke).

Role
Pick the first leaves in early spring and larger leaves as they unfurl in late spring. Pick the spiky buds and flowers for large-scale arrangements later in the year.

Good combinations
Use spring leaves with hellebores, euphorbias and tulips (see page 76). Large summer leaves are perfect with peonies and foxgloves. The flowers are a good foil to sunflowers and on the right scale.

Special growing requirements
Easy to grow in a sunny position. Mulch deeply in autumn. They are robust and quick-growing. You can divide them at the end of every year, artichokes every two. Needs staking.

Delphinium cultivars

1.8m (6ft)
Climate zones 3–7

Description
These tall blue, white or purple spires need no introduction. They are spectacular, summer-flowering plants that no good cutting garden should be without.

Role
Use these as the vertical spire in any large arrangement and use them on their own, stems of different blues erupting in all directions.

Good combinations
Use the blues with any colors, rich or pale (see page 75). The whites look best with other whites and greens, or mixed in with blue.

Special growing requirements
Easy to grow from seed and if sown early, they will produce flowers in the first year. Prone to powdery mildew on the foliage, particularly in a dry year. To maximize their vase life, it's worth internally supporting the hollow stems with a cane once cut. Needs staking.

Eryngium planum, Sea holly

90cm (3ft)
Climate zones 4–8

Description
A small-flowered, blue-stemmed sea holly, which makes a lovely late-summer/autumn garden and cutting plant.

Role
One of the best primary foliage plants you can grow, airy and yet robust, with silvery blue leaves and stems (see page 8).

Good combinations
Perfect with any color, whites and blues, or rich pinks and oranges.

Special growing requirements
Many eryngiums can be tricky to grow, best propagated from root cuttings, but not this one. It's a very easy plant to grow from seed and from an early sowing will go on to flower a little in its first year. Long vase life without any conditioning. Needs staking.

Euphorbia amygdaloides var. *robbiae*

60cm (2ft)
Climate zones 6–9

Description
An evergreen euphorbia with robust, bright acid-green flowers from early March on. This is invaluable for flowering so early and it's an almost indestructible cut flower with a very long vase life.

Role
One of the best spring filler-flowers you can grow. A bit tall and thin in the stem to make the perfect primary foliage, but one not to be without.

Good combinations
Combine it with any color you choose. Mix this with a wallflower and any tulip and you've got a recipe for a hundred different bunches of flowers for spring.

Special growing requirements
This grows almost anywhere – sun, or shade, dry or moist. It will self-seed and may become invasive, so take care where you put it. Sear stem ends to seal in toxic sap. Propagate by division.

Euphorbia characias subsp. *wulfenii*

90cm (3ft)
Climate zones 7–10

Description
Brilliant acid-green batons of flowers with silvery green foliage. This is an evergreen, shrubby plant that looks good every month of the year.

Role
The best base for large arrangements early in the year. The new leaf stems alone are excellent for a large vase at any time of year.

Good combinations
In flower, or not, these are good with any color. For a simple, spectacular arrangement, use five, or seven flowering stems in a large, glass vase with purple honesty (*Lunaria annua*) in between.

Special growing requirements
Needs full sun and good drainage, so on heavy soil add lots of grit and organic material to the planting hole. The flowering spikes should be cut back once they have browned to make room for new growth. This will form next year's flower. Propagate from fresh seed and it self-sows. Transplant seedlings when small as they don't like disturbance. Sear stem ends to seal in toxic sap.

Euphorbia cyparissias

30cm (12in)
Climate zones 4–9

Description
An ideal, small euphorbia for posies. Grow *E. cyparissias* 'Fens Ruby', if you can find it, with red stems beneath characteristic acid-green flowers.

Role
Good foliage base for small arrangements.

Good combinations
This color is good mixed with anything. Combine it with the leaves of *Anthriscus sylvestris* 'Ravenswing'; its crimson leaves highlight the color on the euphorbia stems (see page 77).

Special growing requirements
Tolerant, easy plant that prefers well-drained soil. It can become invasive, spreading by runners, so take care where you site it. Sear stem ends to seal in toxic sap. Propagate by division.

Euphorbia griffithii

90cm (3ft)
Climate zones 4–9

Description
This is the orange-flowered euphorbia. 'Fireglow' is quick growing and can become invasive. 'Dixter' is smaller and more containable. Both are beautiful.

Role
Perfect filler foliage, too floppy to be primary foliage, but invaluable in mid- to late spring. Also turns a good mix of yellows and reds in the autumn.

Good combinations
Mix with an acid-green euphorbia, wallflowers and tulips in crimson, bright pink, purple, or orange (see page 39).

Special growing requirements
Tolerant, easy plant that prefers some moisture in the soil, so add lots of organic material if your soil is light and freely drained. You can divide clumps every couple of years or propagate from semi-ripe cuttings. To do so remove 5cm (2in) long, non-flowering side-branches and push them into a gritty mix of compost. They'll root in a month. Sear stem ends to seal in toxic sap before arranging. Needs staking.

Euphorbia palustris

90cm (3ft)
Climate zones 5–8

Description
Typical bright, euphorbia-green flowers in mid-spring and good tinted foliage in autumn.

Role
Too floppy to be primary foliage, but one of the best filler-foliage plants you can grow; bright, frothy and elegant.

Good combinations
Mix it with any color. It will brighten up whites and blues and highlight the richness of deep reds and purples.

Special growing requirements
Tolerant, easy plant that prefers some moisture in the soil, so add lots of organic material if your soil is light and freely drained. You can divide clumps every couple of years or propagate from semi-ripe cuttings. Cut 5cm (2in) long, non-flowering side-branches and push them into a gritty mix of compost. They'll root in a month. Sear stem ends to seal in toxic sap before arranging. This variety flops without searing. Needs staking.

Euphorbia schillingii

90cm (3ft)
Climate zones 7–9

Description
This late-summer and autumn-flowering euphorbia is one of the best, with characteristic acid-green flowers, larger than most. Very tall and handsome in the garden and the vase.

Role
A perfect basic foliage plant, so grow this in large groups. Like an annual, this euphorbia produces buds below where you cut. These develop into next month's flower.

Good combinations
Use this with any color, bright, or pale. This is a contender to be my favorite foliage plant (see page 124).

Special growing requirements
Easy to grow on almost any soil. You can divide plants every three years and they can also be propagated from semi-ripe cuttings. Remove 5cm (2in) long, non-flowering side branches and push them into a gritty mix of compost. They'll root in a month. Sear stem ends to seal in toxic sap. Needs staking.

Helenium 'Moerheim Beauty'

90cm (3ft)
Climate zones 3–10

Description
Delicious, mahogany-crimson flowers, with a long flowering season for a perennial. If you keep picking these, they keep flowering. Like annuals, if there is a leaf heleniums produce buds below where you cut. These develop into next month's flower.

Role
A perfect bridesmaid or gatecrasher.

Good combinations
This color looks wonderful with large, crimson sunflowers or dahlias. Use it as a gatecrasher with *Cosmos bipinnatus* 'Purity' and white phlox.

Special growing requirements
Easy to grow, a tolerant plant that prefers a site in full sun. It can be divided every two to three years and can be propagated from semi-ripe cuttings, but not every one will root. Needs staking.

Helleborus argutifolius (syn. *H. corsicus*)

60cm (2ft)
Climate zones 6–9

Description
An evergreen hellebore with bright, apple-green flowers and similarly colored seed pods from midwinter to early summer. One of the best all-round perennials.

Role
The Lenten rose, *H. orientalis*, and its hybrids flop when you pick them, but not this one. With *H. argutifolius*, a single, large, floriferous stem makes the perfect base for a medium-sized arrangement and it's excellent filler foliage in spring.

Good combinations
This hellebore has robust, long-lasting flower for mixed arrangements of any color. It's also lovely if you use ten or twenty single flowerheads and float them with night-lights in a large shallow bowl (see page 128).

Special growing requirements
Likes more sun than other hellebores and lots of organic material dug into the soil before planting. Mulch plants in the autumn too. Propagate from fresh seed or division after three or four years.

Lysimachia atropurpurea 'Beaujolais'
60cm (2ft)
Climate zones 3–8

Description
When in bud, these are as glamorous as they come – dark crimson, beaujolais-colored pineapples all the way up the stem. The main bud then elongates and loses its intensity of color, but if you keep picking them, new rich-colored pineapples continue to appear.

Role
One of the best upper story foliage plants you can grow. It will give a dramatic, elegant silhouette to any bunch of flowers (see pages 21 and 139).

Good combinations
I like this color with oranges and apple greens, but try it with whites and creams as well.

Special growing requirements
Very easy to grow from seed and it will flower in its first year from an early sowing. This is one of the perennials that keeps flowering if you keep picking. One of the very best and few people know it. Needs support.

Matthiola, white perennial form
60cm (2ft)
Climate zones 8–10

Description
Silver domes of leaves with white, stock-like flowers held above the foliage. It's not a remarkable looking plant, but its scent is the strongest and most delicious of any plant I know. The perfume is at its most intense at dawn and dusk. One small sprig will fill a room with fragrance.

Role
This is the perfect scent factory for any small arrangement.

Good combinations
Mix it with other whites and crimsons for a powerful scented bunch (see page 68).

Special growing requirements
Easy to grow from seed and will flower in its second year. It's not a long-lived perennial, thriving for only three or four years. As a brassica, it tends to get attacked by shiny, black, flea beetles. This leaves lots of tiny holes in the foliage and flowers. If numbers get out of control, use a physical barrier. I enclose a clump with horticultural fleece.

Nerine bowdenii
60cm (2ft)
Climate zones 9–11

Description
This is a bulbous perennial, superb for flowering in late autumn when every-thing else is brown and gray. It has spectacular flowers – whorls of brilliant pink standing about 60cm (2ft) tall.

Role
This is a bride *par excellence* for an autumn arrangement. They also look good on their own, ten or fifteen stems in a turquoise glass vase.

Good combinations
One of my favorite autumn combinations is nerines mixed with bracken, scabious and *Euphorbia oblongata*.

Special growing requirements
Nerines are easy to grow, but they take ages to get established enough to flower. Just when you've given up on them, four or even five years after planting, they'll appear. Don't buy the more expensive deeper pinks, oranges, or whites. These are not hardy and need overwintering under cover. They need full sun and excellent drainage. Propagate by division.

Paeonia lactiflora cultivars
90cm (3ft)
Climate zones 4–8

Description
Cultivars like 'Shirley Temple' not only look wonderful, but they're scented too. The doubles last better than the single and the Japanese flower forms as above.

Role
These will make any bunch of flowers sumptuous and spectacular. They are also wonderful on their own in a tall, ceramic vase, or float them, with a short section of stem, in a huge, shallow bowl. The jester's hat seedpods look superb as an upper story.

Good combinations
The deep reds are perfect with orange and acid-green. Mix the whites and pale pinks with pastel-colored Iceland poppies and white foxgloves.

Special growing requirements
Peonies take several years to get to a decent size with enough flowers for picking, but they are long-lived, easy perennials. The downside is their short flowering season. Condition by floating in water. Propagate by division.

Phlox paniculata cultivars
90cm (3ft)
Climate zones 4–8

Description
Look out for mildew-resistant, highly scented varieties in almost any color. Choose them when in flower, so you're sure what you're getting. Pick a few stems at a time to prolong flowering and don't cut the stem right to the ground.

Role
Highly scented ingredient for any size arrangement.

Good combinations
Use the purple cultivars, such as 'Amethyst', in a brilliant-colored arrangement of acid-green, orange and purple. Use the whites in huge vases of cosmos, *Nicotiana sylvestris* and euphorbias.

Special growing requirements
The longest lasting cut flowers I grow, with a vase life of three weeks in a cool room. They are easy to grow, with lots of organic material dug in before planting. Mulch in autumn and spring to help retain moisture. Some get mildew on dry soil. Needs staking.

Stipa gigantea
1.5m (5ft) or more
Climate zones 8–10

Description
A tall, elegant grass that looks good throughout the growing season. Bright and golden fresh flowers in late spring or early summer. They gradually dry to a straw-colored crisp in autumn, when they're still lovely covered in frost.

Role
One of the best upper storys you can grow. It also looks superb poking out like sparklers from a hanging globe.

Good combinations
You can mix this with any color.

Special growing requirements
Line your paths with this (see page 14). It is the perfect aisle plant. Plant and divide it in the spring. Until they are well-established, clumps don't like it cold and clammy. For best results. add grit to the soil when you plant.

The essential shrubs

There are also a few shrubs I could not be without; these few really pay their way and so they should, considering the space that they take up!

Daphne odora 'Aureomarginata'

1 x 1m (3 x 3ft)
Climate zones 7–9

Description
This small shrub has a superb fragrance – a clear, spicy, intense citrus scent. It flowers in late winter and early spring when there is little else around.

Role
All you need is two or three sprigs of this to scent a room for a week at a time. The fragrance is magnificent.

Good combinations
Use it on its own, or mix it with early spring flowers.

Special growing requirements
It is slow growing, but easy to strike from cuttings taken in the spring. Will grow in sun or partial shade. A must if you have some room.

Hydrangea macrophylla cultivars

1.5 x 1.5m (5 x 5ft) or more
Climate zones 6–9

Description
This plant has different colored flowers according to the pH of your soil – crimson and pink on alkaline and sky-blue on acid. Both are excellent for late autumn color.

Role
The large pompons make one of the best autumn brides. These are also superb in Christmas wreaths and swags. They keep their color right into the winter.

Good combinations
The turquoise pompons are wonderful with nerines and bright pink dahlias. Use silver birch leaves (as they turn gold), or bracken as your base. Also excellent with wired-in lemons or limes in a Christmas wreath. Use the crimson-flowered forms with clementines.

Special growing requirements
Easy to grow. Cut each flowerhead off just above the first pair of buds beneath it. If the bush gets old and crowded, take out about one in three or four of the oldest shoots at the base in spring, to encourage vigorous new stems.

Hydrangea paniculata 'Grandiflora' and H. arborescens 'Annabelle'
2 x 2m (6 x 6ft)
Climate zones 3–8

Description
Flowers like the snowball bush (*Viburnum opulus* 'Sterile') on steroids. In bud, they are a lovely pale green, opening to creamy white. Perfect for large arrangements.

Role
In bud, a perfect filler foliage. In full flower, one of the best autumn brides or gatecrashers.

Good combinations
Use the buds as a pale-green, brightening filler-foliage with *Atriplex* or *Euphorbia schillingii*. The full flowers are lovely with dark crimson dahlias, such as 'Rip City'.

Special growing requirements
Easy to grow in sun, or part shade. You can cut this right back in winter or early spring without compromising the following season's flowers. Prune each year by cutting back all of the stems to a low woody framework, or right back to the base. They flower best on wood made in the current season.

Rosmarinus officinalis, Rosemary

90 x 90cm (3ft x 3ft)
Climate zones 8–10 (perennial), 3–7 (annual)

Description
Evergreen, silvery green herb that tastes wonderful, looks good in the garden as a hedge or beside an entrance and it's an invaluable picking plant as well. Go for the deep-blue-flowered kinds, such as 'Benenden Blue' or 'Tuscan Blue', for extra color in the spring. 'Jessops Upright' has pale blue flowers but is good for picking with long straight stems.

Role
One of the best plants for winter picking. I use it to decorate candlesticks and swags for Christmas and as a foliage base for spring arrangements (see page 32). It lasts out of water for a few days.

Good combinations
The dark-green leaves need brightening with whites and silvers to look their best. Dark colors get drowned against such a somber backdrop.

Special growing requirements
Easy and quick growing on freely drained soil. In spring, new stems need searing to avoid the tips flopping after a day or two.

Viburnum opulus, Guelder rose

1.8 x 1.8m (6 x 6ft)
Climate zones 2–9

Description
There are two lovely forms of this excellent shrub worth growing: *V. opulus* 'Roseum' or 'Sterile', the snowball bush, covered in flowers in late spring-early summer and even better, with a longer picking season, the straight species, *V. opulus*. This is covered in scarlet to crimson leaves and red, currant-like fruit from late summer till autumn. There is a smaller form, *V. opulus* 'Compactum' and yellow-berried 'Xanthocarpum'.

Role
One of the best late-summer and autumn primary foliage plants. Stems of the berries and turning leaves make a perfect base for any arrangement.

Good combinations
V. opulus is lovely as a base for whites and greens, and equally good with bright and rich colors. I pick this all the time in early autumn. One of my favorite plants.

Special growing requirements
Easy to grow, it likes a moist soil with lots of organic material, but will grow almost anywhere.

spring bulbs

✿ A bulb is a swollen underground food store, rather like an onion, that sends up flowers and leaves each year. The leaves, usually strap-shaped, are there to make as much food as possible to swell the bulb for the next year. The foliage dies down quickly once flowering has finished and the plant enters a dormant period with no signs of life above ground. ✿

A long spring season

Bulbs are more glamorous than this basic description makes out. You have a few early-flowering hardy annuals and biennials, and some excellent leafy perennials to create the foliage bases of your spring arrangements, but the main ingredients to give you strong, intense color, in any shade you want, are bulbs. With their bold shapes, powerful scents, and big blooms, plenty of bulbs in the ground will give you a dressy garden and lots of flowers to bring into the house. You wouldn't have a decent cutting patch without them.

Start by picking narcissi, with cultivars flowering from February into April. Move on to hyacinths, fritillaries, *Anemone coronaria*, and, best of all, tulips to take you through to the middle of May, when there are lots of flowers to choose from. Some tulips have petals with superb, satin textures into the bargain. There is nothing to match the sheen on a dark, crimson-black variety like 'Queen of Night', or the mahogany-red 'Abu Hassan'.

With all these bulbs, if you get them in the ground, they'll flower. They're some of the easiest plants you can grow. You can be a complete gardening ignoramus and bulbs will still fill your patch with color. If you cut open a tulip bulb, you'll see why. The embryonic flower is sitting there, waiting to emerge (see the photograph of a bulb on page 35). All it needs to do is put down a few roots to have a good drink and the flower will start to grow.

Bulbs are not cut-and-come-again. They don't produce more flowers the more you harvest, but most of them are long-lived and you won't have to plant them every year. If you put them in the right place – a sunny spot with good drainage – hyacinths, fritillaries and anemones flower reliably year after year. Narcissi are even easier than that. They'll thrive in partial shade and don't mind a heavy soil. This longevity is not true of all tulips, particularly if you cut them. Hybrids, such as the Parrot tulips, may only keep going for two or three years. They're an extravagance, but not to be missed.

(Opposite) Look at the satiny sheen of this almost black tulip, the wonderful variety 'Queen of Night'.

Picking bulbs

How you pick bulbs plays an important role in how long they last in the garden. All bulbs, whether spring- or summer-flowering, do best if you minimize the number of leaves you cut when you pick the flowers. With narcissi, hyacinths, anemones and alliums, this is easy. Their leaves are in a clump at the bottom, with the flower stems separate, but the leaves of Crown Imperial fritillaries (*Fritillaria imperialis*), tulips, gladioli and lilies also spread up the lower section of the stem. It is important that you don't cut these right to the ground. You need to leave a short section of the leafy part of the stem when cutting to give the bulb a chance to make enough food to survive through the dormant season and produce your flowers for next year.

It's also important to dead-head. If you let any of these plants run to seed, the very formation of the seed diverts energy away from the bulb. This leaves the food store depleted and the whole plant is less likely to survive and flower well the following year. As the blooms go over, if you happen not to have picked them, cut the flowerheads off your bulbs.

All the bulb cultivars I've selected are guaranteed to last well in a vase – these aren't three-day wonders. Once cut, the shortest-lived is the snake's head fritillary (*Fritillaria meleagris*) but it's glamorous and exotic and better for being seen up close. I don't pick huge numbers of them, as I do want them to set seed and self-sow in the garden. Nor do I plant them in my cutting patch. They're happier left undisturbed in grass around an old oak tree, where they thrive on my heavy clay soil. I pick a few heads every week when the plants are in flower.

Narcissi have a reputation of being short-lived as a cut flower, but this isn't true of all of them. The multi-headed, scented flowers of *Narcissus* 'Geranium' last for a week in water in a cool place. If they're picked when the flowers are fresh, *Anemone coronaria*, Crown Imperial fritillaries, hyacinths and tulips will all last a week to ten days in water.

(Below) One of the few narcissi you can pick that will last as long as other plants in a mixed bunch is *Narcissus* 'Geranium'. Make a scented bunch by combining it with white honesty and herbs (see p144).

Choosing spring bulbs

Some types of bulb are better than others for picking and, in some cases, the species or cultivars are classified into a number of groups. But don't be daunted by this; treat it as a useful tool when you're selecting the best for picking.

Anemones

Delicate wood anemones (*Anemone nemorosa*) only last a day or two in water, however you condition them, so are not for the cutting patch. If you cut large-flowered cultivars of *Anemone coronaria* in bud, they will last over a week and they're easy to grow. I prefer the single De Caen Group cultivars to the double St Brigid Group forms. The De Caen Group cultivars are simpler and prettier. Try to find single colors as well. There are several good ones: *A. coronaria* 'The Bride', which is white; 'Orchid', a bright pink; 'Amethyst', blue; and 'Scarlet', which is bright red. The mixed colors have too many muddy, grayish blues and wishy-washy pinks, without the bright clarity of the single-color forms.

Fritillaries

Superb, unusual bulbs that come in a range of sizes from the huge and expensive Crown Imperials (*Fritillaria imperialis*) to the delicate snake's head fritillary (*F. meleagris*). They are becoming more and more widely available year after year in an expanding range of colors and forms.

Hyacinths

Despite their delicious scent, the run-of-the-mill garden hybrid hyacinths (cultivars of *Hyacinthus orientalis*) don't make perfect cut flowers. They have rather clumpy, heavy, drumstick blooms, which are fine if you put a few stems on their own in a vase, but are difficult to combine with other things. If you want them for picking, choose the smallest size in the catalog. These are also the cheapest. Don't buy the more expensive, so-called 'prepared' hyacinths either. These are the heat-treated

ones that you 'force' as early, pot-grown house plants, but it's a waste of money to plant them in the garden as 'forcing' shortens their flowering life.

Look out for Multiflora (also called Roman hyacinths) they're the best for picking. Rather than one huge stem, they have lots of fine stems erupting from one bulb, with fewer, more delicate, individual flowers, more sparsely spaced up the stem. These are better matched to other spring flowers and I prefer them in a vase to their more robust cousins. They are more expensive, a bit harder to find, but really worth the effort.

Narcissus

There are twelve different groups of narcissi, but don't feel overwhelmed when you look at the lists. The big, coarse, trumpety Division 1 and 2 cultivars (Trumpet and Large-cupped Groups) are best planted in lawns. They are chunky and bold and can withstand the competition of the grass, but they look a bit gross in a flowerbed and only last three or four days in a vase before the

(Below) *Tulipa* 'Generaal de Wet' and *Tulipa* 'Negrita' in my cutting garden. I plant tulips in a bed on their own and really pack them in, so I can pick from the patch for three or four years. I never lift my bulbs after planting.

ends of the petals start to brown. They're not around for long enough to justify the space in your cutting patch. Their short vase life also makes them difficult to mix with other flowers. They will be going over when the rest of the bunch is still looking pristine and you'll have to fish them out and leave a hole. The best way to arrange them is in a large glass or ceramic jug on their own.

Narcissi are important in a cutting garden. They're a reliable source of early flowers – a mainstay for March – so, which are the best sorts to plant? Catalog listings often appear under their botanical division. Go for the Triandrus types (Division 5); Cyclamineus (Division 6); Jonquillas (Division 7); Tazettas (Division 8); Poeticus (Division 9); and the species (Division 13); and the smaller-flowered, more delicate kinds in other groups. Many of them have lovely scent and make relatively long-lived cut flowers.

Tulips

Tulips make superb, long-lasting cut flowers. In wet springs, wet-weather tolerance is a real issue with tulips. On the whole, the rich, deep-colored varieties become pock-marked and the petals go spotty in the rain and they look half-finished before they have emerged from bud. Of all the fifteen different tulip groups, the Triumph Group (Division 3), in particular, have good rain resistance and it's worth bearing that in mind.

The catalogs tend to exaggerate the difference in the flowering times of the different groups; they're just covering themselves to take into account the different climatic conditions they might be grown in. With me, the Single Early Group (Division 1) flower only two weeks before the first Parrot tulips (Division 10); the catalogs say that they flower a month apart. But, in any case, if you concentrate your budget on the early and late flowering groups, you can spread your tulip-picking season over at least six weeks, rather than having a tulip bonanza for just a couple of big drum-banging, brouhaha weeks. The Single Earlies are amongst the first to flower and the Single Lates, Viridifloras, Lily-

flowered and Parrots among the last, with the Darwins and Triumphs in between.

Where to buy bulbs

I always recommend buying your bulbs from a mail-order catalog rather than a garden center. They tend to be cheaper by mail order, you have a better selection and they won't have been kept hanging around too long at warm temperatures. Bulb specialists keep their stock at the correct temperature in a cold store until dispatch. This gives the bulbs a much longer shelf life, and although, ideally, you should plant as soon as you get them home, this gives you a few days' grace. If you do buy from a garden center, make sure you buy as soon as the bulbs come in; then they won't have chance to become baked or desiccated before you get them. There are lots of bulb lists, but as a general rule, don't go for the cheapest. In my experience, cheap wholesalers often sell wrongly labelled bulbs. In many cases, what you expect and ordered, does not come up. The more expensive catalogs take more care with their nomenclature.

A healthy bulb is firm, not wrinkly, with the skin still attached. Avoid those that feel soft when you squeeze them and are covered in mildew.

(Below) Healthy tulip bulbs

When to plant

Most spring-flowering bulbs are planted in early autumn. Try and get your narcissi, hyacinths, anemones and fritillaries into the ground in September. These need an extensive root system to flower well, so benefit from being put into the ground as soon as you can.

Tulips are different. They only need to be planted in mid- to late autumn, say October, or even November. They won't start putting down their roots until then. You can put them in earlier, but they will sit there doing nothing. What's more, a few frosts and some cold weather help to wipe out viral and fungal diseases that lurk in the soil and which may infect the bulbs. Planting late is a traditional means of disease protection.

How to plant

Most bulbs have a pointed and a blunt end. Plant them pointy end up. Anemone bulbs are an exception and look like a bit of dried dirt (they're really tubers rather than bulbs). Soak them in a bucket overnight and they will double in size and start growth more quickly than if

planted dry. With anemones, put them with the longest side placed horizontally.

I always plant in clumps or lines of at least twenty-five tulips and anemones, fifteen hyacinths and narcissi and however many I can afford of the fritillaries. Fewer looks fine when they flower the first year, but in subsequent seasons, you get a very dotty effect, which quickly looks messy.

Don't use a bulb planter – it takes too long if you have to make one hole for every bulb. I dig out a trench or shallow hole, taking up as much space as I have room for between other plants. It's just one big hole, dug at the same time, not lots of 'mini-cores'. I then line the hole with grit – nearly all bulbs last longer with good drainage. Place each one at least twice the depth of the bulb (the distance from top to bottom of the bulb) and closer than recommended by most books. This gives a spectacular show in the first year, and it still looks good in the second and third years. If you scatter them at traditional distances of 8–10cm (3–4in) apart, you'll have hardly anything to look at by the third year. Push the bulbs into the grit in the bottom of the trench and then cover them up, mixing more grit into the soil you replace. If you garden on heavy soil, mix in about one-third grit to two-thirds soil. After planting, firm the ground with your hand, not feet, so you don't trample the crowns. This gets rid of any large air pockets. Watering will help this too.

Planting tulips

I plant my tulips in a different way to the rest of my bulbs. They go in later and deeper, in trenches 30cm (12in) wide and deep, with 5cm (2in) of grit lining the bottom. If I'm short of room, I plant the tulips in two layers, one at about 25cm (10in) and one at 15cm (6in), or I plant one layer of tulips and one of something else. The deep layer must always be the tulips. The more superficial layer could be a hyacinth or anemone.

A depth of 25cm (10in) is much deeper than you are usually told to plant tulips, but I've found there are many

(Inset) Cross section of a tulip bulb showing the green flower bud ready to erupt.

My tulip planting system

1 Dig out a trench or round hole, 30cm (12in) deep and 30cm (12in) wide. If you garden on heavy soil, line the bottom of the trench with a 5cm (2in) layer of washed sharp sand or horticultural grit. Add a handful of bonemeal to encourage the formation of next year's flowers and mix it into the soil and sand at the base of the trench.

2 Place the bottom layer of tulips in the trench, 2.5–5cm (1–2in) apart and cover with soil. If you garden on heavy soil, mix the soil with about one-third grit by volume. If you're short of space, put in a second layer of bulbs and cover over with soil mixed with grit. There is still enough soil above the bulbs to allow you to over-plant with biennials in the autumn and half-hardy annuals in early summer without damaging them.

3 Label in pencil and sketch and file a map, just in case. Pencil is less likely than pen to wash off in three or four years and you'll need to know what's growing there for that length of time. If the labels fade, at least you'll have your map to tell you what's what.

advantages to this system. Deeper bulbs are less likely to try and make bulbils (baby bulbs); in shallow soil, the slightly higher temperatures encourage the bulbs' reproduction. As soon as a mother bulb develops little satellites around her base, most of her energy goes into them. The bulb will almost certainly not flower the following year and the bulbils will not be large enough to flower for two or three years after that, so you get a 'blind' bulb. By planting deeply, your tulips won't try to reproduce and are more likely to flower year after year.

With deep planting, you won't need to stake. Even huge bulbs like the tulip 'Ivory Floradale', which can grow to nearly a metre (3ft) tall, with large, heavy flowers, won't need any support to stay vertical. The bulb is anchored so deeply in the ground, it almost never gets blown over.

I started experimenting with deep planting to avoid digging up bulbs all the time when I was putting other plants in over their heads. At 25cm (10in), or even at 15cm (6in) deep, I can plant anything from a 9cm (3½in) pot and the planting hole will still be big enough to take the roots and some organic material. And I still won't have dug up any bulbs. As deep as this, the squirrels and mice won't have a feast either. They don't seem to have the energy to dig this deep. You might try the same technique with narcissus; it works just as well, although they may flower a little later.

After care

It is important to leave the browning foliage on your bulbs until every leaf has died right down, usually by early summer. This allows the plants to photosynthesize for as long as possible, so they store more food in the bulb to produce flowers the following year. This rule applies across the board with bulbs. Some gardeners tie the browning leaves of daffs in a knot to tidy them up as they die down; don't do it – it prevents the products of photosynthesis passing back down the leaves to the bulbs.

People think tulips last better if you lift them and store them to ripen in a light, dry place. A bright shed bench, or laid out on a flattish, hot, shed roof is the perfect place. But I have found that lifting does more damage than good in my garden. I seem to lose more to rot and mildew than when I just leave them in the ground, so unless I have a very rare variety that I'm unlikely to be able to get again, I leave them where they are.

In mid-June, I rake up all the dead foliage and any left-over petals. I then mulch them with 5–8cm (2–3in) of well-rotted manure. They like the nitrogen in the manure and this helps them come back strongly the following year. I over-plant with pot-grown pumpkins, zucchini, half-hardy annual cut flowers, or dahlias, rotating between the three follow-on crops to keep diseases to a minimum.

Treated like this, with low maintenance, I only need to replenish my stock of tulips every three to four years.

The best spring bulbs to grow

You've got to grow a good range of spring bulbs to give your cutting patch and vases color, scale and glamour from early in the year.

Anemone coronaria

30cm (12in)
Climate zones 7–10

Description
Stunning, large, buttercup-like flowers in many colors. The single 'De Caen Group' are more beautiful than the double 'St Brigid Group'.

Role
These make excellent spring bridesmaids to a tulip bride. They are one of the longest-lasting spring cut flowers you can grow. A generous vase of 20 or 30 stems of anemones on their own looks good for 10 days.

Good combinations
If you force them early, arrange the deep pink with snake's head fritillaries (see the arrangement on page 135). The deep blue is good with orange, the white with the tulip 'Spring Green'.

Special growing requirements
Easy to grow in full sun, in a sheltered spot with good drainage. They are excellent for forcing under cover in a cold frame or greenhouse to give flowers from February onwards. In the garden, they flower late April/May.

Fritillaria imperialis, Crown Imperial

90cm (3ft)
Climate zones 4–6

Description
These fritillaries are the most glamorous flowers of the spring cutting garden – handsome, impressive and grand. They do have an odd, slightly oniony or foxy smell. Wonderful seed pods too, which should be cut before the bulb puts energy into making seeds.

Role
This makes a spectacular bride for mid-spring arrangements and is an amazing sight, just one stem in a tall, glass vase.

Good combinations
One of the highlights of spring is yellow Crown Imperials arranged with emerging, bright acid-green, spring leaves and stripy yellow and red *Tulipa* 'Mickey Mouse' or 'Flaming Parrot'.

Special growing requirements
They like a site in full sun, with lots of organic material added to the soil to help retain moisture in a hot summer. They flower for two or three years in a shadier spot, but will not live as long without sun. They are one of the few bulbs that do well on a heavy soil. Needs staking.

Fritillaria meleagris, Snake's head fritillary

15cm (6in)
Climate zones 4–8

Description
I love this well-known, elegant, checkered flower in plum-purple or white.

Role
Use this as a bride in a small mixed posy (see the arrangement on page 135), or collect several stems on their own for looking at close-up. Place a vase beside your bed or on your desk.

Good combinations
Exotic and glamorous blooms however you use them.

Special growing requirements
A small bulb that prefers a heavy soil, self-sowing as a wild flower in damp meadowland. Sear the stem ends to maximize its vase life. Don't pick all your flowers as this bulb self-sows.

Hyacinthus orientalis 'Jan Bos'

15–20cm (6–8in)
Climate zones 4–8

Description
An intense, bold pink hyacinth that flowers earlier than most at the beginning of April. Fantastic scent.

Role
This has short stems, but still makes a spectacular bride. Or put it in a vase on its own for your bedside table. It will last at least a week in water, pouring out scent.

Good combinations
For a mixed bunch, combine it with orange tulips like 'Prinses Irene' and 'Generaal de Wet', the orange wallflower, *Erysimum cheiri* 'Fire King' and acid-green euphorbias.

Special growing requirements
Hyacinths are easy, reappearing reliably year after year. Like all bulbs, they thrive in soil with good drainage, so add grit if you garden on heavy soil.

Hyacinthus, multiflowered blue

15cm (6in)
Climate zones 4–8

Description
This is the dark, rich blue version of 'Multiflora White'. Flowers in late April.

Role
Lovely in mixed arrangements with other delicate spring flowers.

Good combinations
Perfect for arranging with *Narcissus* 'Geranium' for a highly scented bedside table vase. I also like these in a series of small glasses, seven or nine stems in each, down the middle of a table.

Special growing requirements
You treat these as you would the *Hyacinthus orientalis* cultivars, choosing a sunny spot and adding grit to the soil. They can be shorter lived than the other type.

Hyacinthus,
multiflowered white

15cm (6in)
Climate zones 4–8

Description
A white Multiflora hyacinth that looks more like a glamorous, large-flowered bluebell than a hyacinth. It flowers in late April. Multiflora types are my favorite for picking.

Role
Lovely in mixed arrangements with other delicate spring flowers.

Good combinations
Use them with spring snowflakes, *Leucojum vernum*, *Dicentra spectabilis* 'Alba' and white narcissi for a delicate and fragrant vase.

Special growing requirements
You treat these as you would the *Hyacinthus orientalis* cultivars, choosing a sunny spot and adding grit to the soil. They can be shorter lived than the other type.

Hyacinthus 'Woodstock'

15–20cm (6–8in)
Climate zones 4–8

Description
My favorite hyacinth, with flowers the color of beetroot juice running out over a white plate. Fantastic scent. Flowers slightly later than *H.* 'Jan Bos' in mid April. It's very similar to *H. orientalis* 'Distinction'.

Role
Another good bride and perfect on its own in an acid-green, purple or turquoise glass.

Good combinations
Mix it with almost any early tulip. This cultivar looks lovely in a bedside table arrangement with other spring flowers – *Anthriscus sylvestris* 'Ravenswing', euphorbias and orange Iceland poppies (see the arrangement on page 77).

Special growing requirements
Hyacinths are easy, reappearing reliably year after year. Like all bulbs, they thrive in soil with good drainage, so add grit if you garden on heavy soil.

Narcissus poeticus

40cm (16in)
Climate zones 4–8

Description
(Division 9, Poeticus)
This is my favorite narcissus for planting in drifts in the grass. The flowers are beautiful – large but delicate, with white petals around a small yellow cup with a bright red, pencil line around its edge. It has a strong, sweet scent. It's very close to the species, *N. poeticus*, the Poet's or Pheasant's eye narcissus

Role
There's almost nothing better in spring than a huge white jug filled with forty or fifty stems of these. The vase will last a week and it will fill the house with scent.

Good combinations
Good on their own.

Special growing requirements
Another easy narcissus that thrives in grass or border, in sun or partial shade.

Narcissus 'February Gold'

30cm (12in)
Climate zones 4–8

Description
(Division 6, Cyclamineus)
A fine, golden narcissus with petals swept right back behind a narrow trumpet.

Role
Invaluable for its early flowering. This is the first flower I can pick and I have a whole glass vase of it at the very beginning of spring.

Good combinations
Its golden color is good with hellebores in black-crimson or white.

Special growing requirements
An easy narcissus that thrives in grass, or border, in sun or partial shade.

Narcissus 'Geranium'

35cm (14in)
Climate zones 4–8

Description
(Division 8, Tazetta)
A sweetly scented narcissus with white petals around an orange cup, multi-headed, with four or five flowers on top of every stem. Blooms in April with the first of the tulips.

Role
Out of all the narcissi I've grown, this lasts the longest in a vase, looking good for a week. Fill a glass with it alone, or mix it with other spring flowers.

Good combinations
This makes a wonderful bridesmaid with a white hyacinth, or a Single Early white tulip. It's also good arranged with rosemary and early spring herbs, filled out with clouds of white honesty (see the arrangement on page 32).

Special growing requirements
Another easy narcissus that thrives in grass or border, in sun or partial shade.

Narcissus 'Tête-à-Tête'

20cm (8in)
Climate zones 4–8

Description
(Division 12, Miscellaneous group)
A miniature narcissus with egg-yolk yellow flowers. They bloom early, from mid-March. Lovely in small drifts in the garden and an excellent form for forcing. Once planted in a pot, they re-emerge year after year with no upkeep.

Role
Best on their own, or as a bride in an early spring arrangement. If picked in bud, they last in water for five to six days.

Good combinations
They look good with hellebores and the first cardoon leaves, or arrange them in a small glass vase with deep purple, winter-flowering pansies.

Special growing requirements
These are very easy to grow and will be happy in sun, or partial shade. They are best planted in a border – they can't compete with grass.

37

Narcissus 'Thalia'

30cm (12in)
Climate zones 4–8

Description
(Division 5, Triandrus)
Creamy-white flowers,
with clusters of three
or four blooms at the
top of every stem.
Elegant and fine, with
a faint, sweet scent.
Flowers in early April.

Role
Tall and impressive
enough to mix into a
tied spring bunch, or
pick twenty stems to
arrange on their own
for a jug on the
kitchen table.

Good combinations
Lovely with blossom,
pussy willow and
euphorbia, or in
contrast to dark tulips
and the wallflower,
Erysimum cheiri
'Blood Red'.

**Special growing
requirements**
Another easy
narcissus that thrives
in grass or border, in
sun or partial shade.

Tulipa 'Abu Hassan'

45cm (18in)
Climate zones 4–7

Description
(Division 3, Triumph.
These are tall,
handsome tulips with
excellent weather
resistance.) This has
delicious sheeny,
deep mahogany-red
flowers. A fine,
sophisticated plant
and one of the
darkest colors, yet
the petals don't mark
in the rain.

Role
Good for arranging on
its own.

Good combinations
This color is
wonderful with the
orange-flowered
Euphorbia griffithii and
contrasting, bright
acid-green *Euphorbia
palustris*.

**Special growing
requirements**
An easy, long-lived,
mid-season tulip.
Expect this to flower
in late April.

Tulipa acuminata

50cm (20in)
Climate zones 4–7

Description
(Division 15,
Miscellaneous and
Species tulips)
A weird and wonderful
tulip that is like a
spider turned on its
head. Yellow and red
petals.

Role
Add to arrangements
as an upper story. It
has the best
silhouette of any
spring flower.

Good combinations
Use it for each and
every mixed spring
bunch.

**Special growing
requirements**
An easy tulip that
appears reliably year
after year. It must
have full sun and
good drainage.

Tulipa 'Artist'

45cm (18in)
Climate zones 4–7

Description
(Division 8, Viridiflora.
All of the Viridifloras
have green in their
flowers; some are
entirely green, others
rimmed or flamed with
another color.) This
is a bold orange
viridiflora, with green
centers to every petal.
It's excellent for
containers, standing
only 45cm (18in) tall,
so it doesn't flop.

Role
A very versatile tulip
which is lovely in
almost any
combination in the
garden or the vase.

Good combinations
Orange goes well with
almost any color –
white and green, blue,
purple or deep red.
Use it as the
bridesmaid with
'Ballerina', as the
bride with early
orange marigolds or
just in a duo with blue
autumn-sown
cornflowers which
should be in flower at
the same time.

**Special growing
requirements**
It's the most perennial
tulip I've grown,
coming up every year
in my garden from a
planting seven years
ago and it is unusual
in that it thrives in
partial shade.

Tulipa 'Apricot Parrot'

50cm (20in)
Climate zones 4–7

Description
(Division 10, Parrot
tulips. The most
flamboyant group of
all, with large, frilly
flowers.) Pale apricot
and butterscotch are
not my colors, but this
is a stunning tulip.
The outside of the
flowers starts strong
orange. They fade as
they age to a pale
orange-pink.

Role
Pick them on their
own for arranging in a
blue glass vase, or
mix them with whites
and greens.

Good combinations
Lovely with lots of
white honesty and
cardoon leaves.

**Special growing
requirements**
This variety lasts well
over a week in water,
looking better and
better. The stems do
the classic, swan-
neck twist. Expect this
to flower at the
beginning of May.

Tulipa 'Ballerina'

55cm (22in)
Climate zones 4–7

Description
(Division 6, Lily-
flowered. These are
the most elegant,
pointed petalled tulips
with a slim silhouette.
They are the cat-walk
models of the tulip
world.) Supremely
elegant, deep orange
tulip with a sweet,
freesia-like scent. This
one is a real favorite
of mine.

Role
The perfect bride in a
bold, spring
arrangement.

Good combinations
Mix this with a
euphorbia base,
T. 'Generaal de Wet'
or orange calendulas
as the bridesmaid
and *T.* 'Mariette' as
the gatecrasher.

**Special growing
requirements**
Expect this to flower
at the start of May.

(Opposite)
A spring vase
(see p144).

Tulipa 'Black Parrot'

55cm (22in)
Climate zones 4–7

Description
(Division 10, Parrot tulips) I love Parrot tulips. They are cultivars that look marvellous fully blown, with stems twisting all over the place and some petals dropping onto the table. This is one of my favorites, with shaggy, cut edges to every petal and some green stripes on the outside.

Role
Wonderful as a bride or on their own in a vase of acid-green *Euphorbia palustris* or *Helleborus corsicus*.

Good combinations
Perfect as the bride in a huge globe with *T.* 'Queen of Night' as the bridesmaid and orange tulips as the gatecrasher.

Special growing requirements
This is one of the shortest-lived of tulips, flowering well for two or three years. Expect it to flower at the beginning of May.

Tulipa 'Flaming Parrot'

55cm (22in)
Climate zones 4–7

Description
(Division 10, Parrot tulips) Amazing huge flowers, pale-yellow with red ripples. *T.* 'Texas Flame' (see page 133) is similar, but even bigger and with a brighter yellow base. It flowers two weeks later. Think Dutch still life with both these bulbs.

Role
Good when fifteen or twenty stems are arranged on their own.

Good combinations
For a lavish arrangement, mix 'Flaming Parrot' with the last of the yellow Crown Imperial fritillaries. Their flowering season will just overlap.

Special growing requirements
This cultivar lasts well over a week in water, looking better and better. The stems do the classic, swan-neck twist. Expect it to flower at the beginning of May.

Tulipa 'Gavota'

45cm (18in)
Climate zones 4–7

Description
(Division 3, Triumph) Tall, slim flowers in deep mahogany-red, fading gradually to a golden edge. A new cultivar that is one of my favorites.

Role
Lovely in a mixed bunch and I use this as a single stem on its own (see the arrangement on page 28).

Good combinations
Similar coloring, but a different shape to 'Abu Hassan', so put these together with an acid-green base.

Special growing requirements
An easy, long-lived, mid-season tulip. Expect this to flower in late April.

Tulipa 'Generaal de Wet'

40cm (16in)
Climate zones 4–7

Description
(Division 1, Single Early) A yellow-based, red-washed tulip that looks orange from afar. It has a delicious, sweet, freesia-like scent. This is one of my favorites and is useful for flowering early in April.

Role
Lovely in a mixed bunch of intense, rich-colored spring flowers.

Good combinations
I mix this with deep pink, purple, or dark crimson tulips and acid-green euphorbias.

Special growing requirements
An easy, long-lived tulip that flowers earlier than most. – expect it in mid April.

Tulipa 'Groenland', syn. 'Greenland'

40cm (16in)
Climate zones 4–7

Description
(Division 8, Viridiflora) Pink petals with lots of green overlaid. The best-selling tulip on my spring bulb list.

Role
A marvellous tulip on its own and it mixes well with white, pale pink, soft orange and green.

Good combinations
Beautiful as a bridesmaid to the deep-pink Lily-flowered tulip, 'Mariette'. For a calm vase, add a white gatecrasher. For some zing, add orange.

Special growing requirements
This has a long vase and garden life. You can't really beat this tulip. Expect it to flower in early May.

Tulipa 'Ivory Floradale'

70cm (28in)
Climate zones 4–7

Description
(Division 4, Darwin Hybrid. Great big tulips - the rugby-players of the tulip world.) The flowers of this tulip look like ostrich eggs on stems – huge, cream spheres with an occasional fleck of carmine.

Role
The flowers are large enough to fill my cupped hands. Spectacular on their own in a tall glass vase.

Good combinations
They also look good with cardoon leaves – spiky and silver – mixed in with the flowers.

Special growing requirements
You won't need any stakes or support if you plant this giant 23cm (9in) deep in the soil. Expect flowers at the beginning of May.

Tulipa 'Mariette'

60cm (24in)
Climate zones 4–7

Description
(Division 6, Lily-flowered) There are two pink Lily-flowered tulips that I love: 'China Pink', a pale shade, and 'Mariette', which is almost magenta. This is my favorite – large flowers in an intense, saturated color.

Role
This makes a spectacular bride.

Good combinations
Mix it with orange *T.* 'Ballerina', for a strong contrast, or match it with a bridesmaid, *T.* 'Groenland', a pink-rimmed Viridiflora.

Special growing requirements
Expect this to flower at the start of May.

Tulipa 'Mickey Mouse'

40cm (16in)
Climate zones 4–7

Description
(Division 1, Single Early) A horrid name for a lovely tulip – yellow with red, raspberry-ripple markings. Excellent for the brave.

Role
This makes any bunch of flowers look like a Dutch still-life painting.

Good combinations
Best with other tulips – deep reds, and purples.

Special growing requirements
An easy, long-lived tulip that flowers earlier than most. Expect this to be in full bloom in mid-April.

Tulipa 'Orange Favorite'

55cm (22in)
Climate zones 4–7

Description
(Division 10, Parrot tulips) Fantastic, brilliantly frilly orange tulip with splashes of green and purple on the outside. It has a lovely freesia-like scent.

Role
The perfect bride.

Good combinations
Mix it with orange marigolds as the bridesmaids and crimson or pink tulips as the gatecrasher. It's also lovely with the *Allium hollandicum* 'Purple Sensation', which flowers at the same time.

Special growing requirements
Along with *T.* 'Texas Flame' this flowers later than any other tulip. Invaluable for extending your tulip season.

Tulipa 'Queen of Night'

60cm (24in)
Climate zones 4–7

Description
(Division 5, Single Late) One of the most handsome tulips, with almost black flowers and a perfect, satiny sheen. The flowers are large and stems long.

Role
Use this in a mixed arrangement with lots of other tulips. This cultivar gets clear-felled, not a single stem left unpicked, in the cutting garden at home.

Good combinations
Contrast this with creams and whites, or mix it with the deep-red wallflower, *Erysimum cheiri* 'Blood Red', orange tulips and Iceland poppies. A wonderful bride or gatecrasher.

Special growing requirements
Well-known mid-season tulip. Sadly, this cultivar has poor weather resistance and the buds and flowers will spot if it pours with rain. Expect this to flower at the start of May.

Tulipa 'Spring Green'

50cm (20in)
Climate zones 4–7

Description
(Division 8, Viridiflora) Creamy-white flowers with stripes of green on the outside. They look good in bud, flower and even as they age.

Role
These green-flashed tulips make fantastic fillers with other flowers.

Good combinations
Use this as the bridesmaid with other whites, or as a gatecrasher with pink and apricot (see the arrangement on page 76).

Special growing requirements
Superb, very perennial tulips that reappear reliably for year after year. They also have one of the longest vase lives. More expensive than others, but well worth it. Expect this to flower in early May.

Tulipa 'White Triumphator'

70cm (28in)
Climate zones 4–7

Description
(Division 6, Lily-flowered) This is the best white tulip you can grow. It's tall, elegant and pure white.

Role
A good bride and lovely on its own.

Good combinations
Mix it with other whites, or contrast with dark reds and crimsons.

Special growing requirements
Expect this to flower at the start of May.

hardy annuals

 An annual is a plant that lives for one year, forming roots, leaves, flowers and seed all within twelve months. Hardy annuals withstand winter cold, and will survive with foliage above ground through the frosts. Without hardy annuals, the cutting patch would be completely lost.

The mainstay of your patch

Hardy annuals are the backbone and the glory of everything that you will do in your patch – adaptable, glamorous, easy, cheap and productive. I know the phrase 'hardy annual' seems a bit dull and off-putting, but ignore that and think instead of what these flowers can do for you.

Hardy annuals should fill a major part of your cutting patch. They are not to be missed. They'll thrive in almost any soil, as long as you can find them a spot in the sun. Sow them straight into the ground – all you need is some bare soil, a packet of seed, a spade and a rake. That's it – no greenhouses, propagators, or cold frames. It's as simple as it comes – an absolute beginner or a child can do it.

Infinite variety

You've got straightforward, simple flowers like *Ammi majus*, a lacy, delicate, long-lived version of cow parsley. My favorite arrangement of early summer is a globe of this all on its own (see page 49). There are also corn poppies in soft colors – pink, silver, white and mauve, as well as red. People think poppies don't last if you pick them, but if you sear the stem ends (see page 131) and keep the vase out of drafts, they won't flop or drop their petals for four or five days. I love them, fifteen or twenty stems in a glass vase on the kitchen table, standing in the middle of a pile of petal confetti. Don't clear the petals up straight away. Leave them where they drop until they begin to brown.

There are some truly luxurious, glamorous hardy annuals as well as those which resemble wild flowers. The large, deep-red sunflowers (*Helianthus annuus* 'Deep Red') are spectacular in the garden and in a vase. They are the color of dark chocolate with crimson mixed in, and the petals have a texture of the best silk velvet. Arrange them with a sharp color – gold or acid-green. I often put them with clouds of dill (*Anethum graveolens*). The dill is like the lemon with smoked salmon - you need its acidity to cut through the richness of the rest (see opposite).

(Opposite below) Delicate but long-lasting *Ammi majus* with the black *Scabiosa atropurpurea* 'Black Cat'.

(Below) *Helianthus annuus* 'Deep Red' with *Nigella hispanica* seedpods both set against acid-green dill.

(Overleaf) A self-perpetuating bedding scheme of hardy annuals: *Nigella hispanica* and *Calendula* 'Indian Prince'.

Black beauties

I'm keen on nearly black flowers. Black goes well with almost everything. You can combine it with whites and creams and it looks dramatic; or you can mix it with other strong, saturated colors – orange, gold and Moroccan blue – for a sumptuous Venetian vase. I always grow lots of the black cornflower (*Centaurea cyanus* 'Black Ball'). It's in bloom for longer and lasts better in water than the blue, and the flowers don't bleach out as they age. I grow half a row of this, with a quarter red and a quarter blue.

The very dark, annual scabious (*Scabiosa atropurpurea*) is another wonderful near-black flower. It has the same velvet texture as the sunflower and blooms for longer than any other annual I know. It's really a short-lived perennial that produces most flowers in its first year. Its perennial status means it's slow to get going and you won't have flowers from an autumn sowing until midsummer, but its beauty lasts into late autumn, when there is very little else around. I've even picked them on Christmas day from plants in a sheltered spot.

And thinking of winter, don't forget pansies (*Viola*). If you sow these in early autumn (early September) and put them in pots around your door in October or November, you'll have almost black flowers to pick in late winter and early spring (February and March). I arrange them in small glasses with aconites, crocus and golden narcissi, such as *Narcissus* 'Tête-à-Tête'.

Perpetual profusion

Many hardy annuals self-sow. If you've put them into your garden once, you won't need to sow again. They're self-perpetuating and that's a joy. It's one less thing to do in spring. They'll appear around where you had plants last year. You can leave them where they are, thinning them out so they have enough room to bulk up, or transplant them into your cutting patch. Before moving them, soak the roots with a sprinkler for at least an hour. Dig them up with a trowel, keeping as much soil as you can in a good 8–10cm (3–4in) root ball. Water them in well in their new place. This minimizes root disturbance

and the seedlings won't falter with the move.

Self-sown seedlings will give you plenty of cut flowers for early summer picking, but you can bring this date a month forward by making supplementary sowings straight into the ground in early autumn. Plants sown then will flower from mid-May, which can be a difficult time, with little around for picking. The tulips have ended and there is nothing yet to take their place. Autumn-sown hardy annuals plug this gap and there are some, like *Cerinthe major* and *Euphorbia oblongata*, which will flower from mid-March onwards. These give you invaluable bulk early in the year.

Which hardy annuals to grow

To have the right balance in your cutting patch, you need equal quantities of foliage and flowers. This is a mistake that lots of people make. They think they've got plenty of foliage from shrubs and perennials in the rest of the garden, are tempted by glamorous blooms – the sunflowers, sweet peas and scabious – and fill up their patches with them. Don't fall into this trap. Make at least 50 per cent of your plants foliage filler and upper-story foliage plants for the best arrangements.

How to grow hardy annuals

Growing hardy annuals is easy, but I have six key points that I always stick to because they guarantee success.

1 Don't sow too early

Imagine you're a seed sown into cold, damp soil with more dark hours than light, and under gray skies. What happens? You sit there with your thick carapace firmly in place. The most likely thing is that you rot away in the wet, or are eaten by the birds. Sown too early, you'll end up with a very patchy row. Contrast this to being sown into soil that is beginning to warm up. It reaches 7–10°C (45–50°F) and has dried out a bit. There are more than twelve hours of daylight and the skies are bright. You germinate quickly and life is viable.

You'll know when the sowing moment has arrived without looking at the calendar. All over the garden, seedlings are appearing. Many of them will be weeds, but there will be seedlings from annual plants you want in the garden too. Poppies, dill, marigolds, cerinthe and bupleurum will be popping up like mustard and cress. This is the best sign that conditions for sowing outside are right. If nature's doing it, you do it too.

2 Prepare the soil

Sow into soil with a fine consistency, with lumps no bigger than a damson. Again, imagine it from the seed's point of view. The seed carries a small amount of stored food – just enough to keep it going until it reaches the light and starts making its own. Once the seedling is photosynthesizing, it's almost certainly away, and able to make as much food as it needs to grow.

But if seed has been sown into heavy, sticky soil with clods the size of grapefruits, its journey will be hard. The emerging shoot hits a large clod and can't push its way through. The only way to the light is the long way round; the shoot gets half way up – still underground and in the dark – and runs out of food. That's it, it's over. The nascent seedling shrivels and dies.

Contrast this to a seed sown into crumbly soil with small particles and of fine consistency. If it's lucky, there's lots of easily penetrated organic matter and, even better, some grit, which it can creep its way between. Within days of germination, the shoot pushes through the crumbly soil, straight up and out into the light. Large seeds, say sunflower or marigold, stand a better chance than most. There's more starch in the seeds, so they can survive a longer journey in a coarser terrain. With the fine seeds, like those of cornflowers, forget it. If the soil is like that on a building site, they won't stand a chance.

But there's another side to this coin. Large seeds have large surface areas and in wet soil, they're more likely to rot. They can't afford to hang around in a cold, clammy soil for long. Small seed will be fine, surviving for months, even years, in anything but a sodden bog.

You've got to work the soil to create that perfect consistency, if you want to succeed with sowing directly into the ground. It won't take years, as many people think. It's more like a few hours with several wheelbarrow loads of well-rotted manure or garden compost, perhaps some grit if you're on heavy soil, and a rototill by your side – the easy recipe for an almost instant perfect conditions.

3 Don't sow too thickly

Sow as thinly as you can. Take individual seeds (if large, like calendulas) or a pinch of seed (if small, like poppies) from your palm and sow as finely as you can into shallow drills, no more than 1–2cm (½–¾in) deep. The ideal spacing is 5cm (2in) apart – impossible with tiny seeds.

(Opposite) This is one of my favorite early summer arrangements – a globe of *Ammi majus* (see p144).

For small seeds, sow quickly; a small pinch at a time. I promise this gives you a thinner distribution of seed than if you're meticulous and slow. Mark where you've got to with each pinch, so you don't miss a bit, or sow in the same soil twice. I make a line with my finger across the drill.

Don't pour straight from the packet, or the crease in the palm of your hand. This creates clumps of seed in one place, with lots of tiny plants competing for light, food and water, then bare patches in between. And don't go back over the line once you've sown, chucking a few more seeds in for good measure. You're just adding more competition for the seeds already there. Care taken now is time saved later.

4 Thin-out the seedlings

Seeds start to germinate after about a week and tiny seedlings appear. When the seedlings are about 2.5cm (1in) tall and have at least two pairs of leaves, one that looks like a tiny version of those of the parent plant, get brutal. Thin them out, leaving one good plant every 10cm (4in). It's crucial you do this; seedlings won't do well with too much competition from close neighbors.

At this stage, they're usually too small to transplant. Just pull the seedlings up by the roots and chuck them. Beginners find this difficult – it feels like infanticide. It's exciting when things start to appear and it seems such a waste to chuck three-quarters of them away, but it's essential for the seedlings' success. Firm the soil back around the roots of the plants still in the ground and water to settle them back into the soil.

5 Thin again

Thin again to the final planting distance as instructed on the back of the seed packet. Give them plenty of room. I have experimented with different thinning distances and found that spacing for most average-sized hardy annuals should be 25–30cm (10–12in), and for larger ones, 45–50cm (18–20in). This is more generous than is usually recommended, but I've found that the more

(Below) A low-maintenance system of support: green plastic pea netting stretched between bamboo canes. The plants grow through the mesh and hide it within weeks.

room you give them, the more leaf they make. This increases their potential for photosynthesis. They then produce more flowers and live longer. If you crowd plants, the undue competition makes them feel that death is near. Before filling out, they'll quickly run up to flower and produce seed so they can reproduce. This is not what you want – the aim is to get them to live as long as possible to maximize the crop.

By this stage, the seedlings are large enough – and the root structure sufficiently established – to survive being dug up and planted somewhere else. Take about half of them out; leave the first and fourth plants in the row, and transplant the second and third somewhere else, and so on. Water well before you do this and water the transplants into their new home.

Leave this second thinning until the spring if your plants are autumn-sown. You will inevitably lose a few seedlings in the autumn and if you thin too soon after sowing you'll have gaps in your row.

(Below) Take a piece of string 50cm (8in) long. Start by making the two loops (step 1) then tuck the left behind the right and slip over the cane (step 2). Finish by fastening to the cane with a figure eight knot (step 3).

6 Provide support

It's important to stake and support all of your plants. It's crucial to maximize stem length and productivity. If you don't, all but the smallest blow over in the wind or rain. Within twenty-four hours, the growing tip turns up towards the light and develops a bend in the stem. This makes them almost impossible to use in the vase and you end up with a short stem, wasting lots of length.

The simplest and least time-consuming support system, ideal for fine-stemmed flowers, such as cornflowers and nigella, is to stretch netting tightly between canes, spaced 1m (3ft) apart, down either side of the row or group. Tie the netting to the canes with twine. Attach one layer of netting at 30–45cm (12–18in) and another layer about 30cm (12in) above that, if the plants are taller (see pages 16–17).

If you use green plastic pea-netting, with a large 5–8cm (2–3in) gauge, you won't notice it. The plastic quickly gets hidden by foliage and flowers and yet there is enough support to stop the row being bashed to the ground in any but major storms.

With stout-stemmed, large-flowered plants, such as dahlias and sunflowers, you will need individual stakes. For larger plants use robust bamboo. Place the cane about 5cm (2in) from the bottom of the main stem of the plant.

The clove hitch knot is perfect for staking. Once attached, it stays exactly where you put it, never slipping down to the ground. This is the system to use. Attach your string to the cane with a clove hitch knot (see below, left) and then tie it onto the plant with a figure eight. Don't pull the stem tight up to the cane, or it will snap. The figure eight means that there's a layer of string to act as a buffer between the stem and cane and it gives more support than a straight loop.

A clove hitch knot with a figure of eight

1

2

3

Preparing the ground

In an ideal world, you will have dug over the ground well before sowing to incorporate well-rotted organic material: garden compost or manure. Do it in the autumn if you garden on clay, or in late winter or early spring – about a month or so before sowing – if your soil is sandy or chalky. If you garden on poorly drained clay soils, add grit or horticultural sharp sand as well. On this sort of soil, leave large lumps where they are over winter – the frost will help break them down.

Get rid of all annual and perennial weeds as you dig. If you think your soil may be thick with ungerminated annual weed seed, cover it with clear plastic for two weeks before sowing. This encourages the first flush of annual weeds to germinate. Hoe them off and compost them. Once the soil has been dug, try not to tread on it – this will compact the soil and squeeze all the vital, moisture- and air-holding spaces out of it, damaging the structure. To distribute your weight evenly over the area, stand on a plank of wood.

Choose a dry day, preferably following a couple of days of dry weather, to prepare the ground for sowing.

Thump any large lumps of soil with the back of a metal rake. They'll shatter when dry, but remain cloddy when wet. Work out where your rows are going to be and fine tune the soil in these places only. Don't try to get every last inch of the patch to a perfect consistency; it makes unnecessary work. Rake in one direction, drawing lumps bigger than a damson to the side; then repeat at right angles. This should create a perfect, fine tilth with the consistency of apple-crumble topping, but only in a narrow band. The lumps at either side will help inhibit weed seed germination.

There are some plants, such as dill, cerinthe and bupleurum, that thrive in a poor, freely drained soil. I garden on heavy clay, so I add a couple of wheelbarrows of grit to areas where I will be sowing these. It makes all the difference to germination.

Sowing seed

I never broadcast seed free-style. It's best to sow in rows or blocks of rows. You'll know that the seedlings that appear in lines are the plant you've sown. Those outside the line are likely to be weedlings and can be removed. Go for blocks if you're integrating the flowers into your borders. I like the allotment feel of rows if you're creating a separate patch.

To sow in rows, mark them out with string, or fine, horticultural silver sand. Dry the sand out and pour it from a bottle. This also makes the sowing line clear as the seedlings germinate and is a good thing to do until you gain confidence. Straight lines look much better than wavy ones, so it's worth using canes and string to create a line rather than doing it by eye.

To sow in blocks, mark out a series of short parallel lines, travelling diagonally across the block, 30cm (12in) apart (check spacings on the back of the seed packet). Alternatively, sow in a checkered grid. With either of these systems, the rows merge into a block within four to six weeks and will lose any military neatness. Use silver sand to mark your lines. Canes and string would be a fussy business.

(Opposite) *Cerinthe major* '**Purpurascens**' **with the poppy,** *Eschscholzia californica* '**Orange King**'.

(Below) **I use Moroccan tea glasses for small, individual arrangements like** *Calendula* '**Touch of Red**' **mix.**

Drag the handle of your rake or trowel along the row to make a shallow drill, 1–2cm (½–¾in) deep. There is a general rule that you sow seed at a depth related to the size of the seed. Large sunflower seeds should be pushed in about 2.5cm (1in) deep with your finger. Tiny poppy seeds should be almost surface-sown, with only the lightest covering of soil to stop them from being displaced by watering. Again, check the seed packet for sowing details.

Water the trench before sowing. It speeds up germination and means you won't have to water after sowing and risk displacing the seeds. The warm soil that you will push back over the seeds acts like a cloche. The seed then experiences the perfect conditions for quick germination – warm, dark and moist. Sow the seed as thinly as you can. Replace the soil by hand and, with the palm of your hand, pat it down firmly all the way along the row. This helps the seeds make intimate contact with the soil and speeds up their germination.

Aftercare

If there is no rain, water twice a week. Don't just give a quick sprinkle, but really wet the ground to a depth of several inches. This encourages the roots to follow the water and the plants will form deep, strong roots. After a couple of weeks, the roots will have reached the ground water in most soils, and so I stop watering unless there's a prolonged period of drought.

The seedlings must be kept free of weeds, which will compete for light, food and water and do your plants no good. Regular hoeing is the best method with annual weeds. Some weeds, such as chickweed and bitter cress, set seed and spread very quickly, so be vigilant about these. The best time to hoe is early in the morning on a hot, dry day. The hoed weeds will quickly shrivel up in the sun. You'll still need to hand weed in between the plants, because hoeing may damage roots.

After hoeing, I apply a 5cm (2in) layer of mulch. You need to wait until the seeds have germinated and the

rows and groups are clearly visible. Mulches cut down the effort needed for weeding by three-quarters, by preventing light reaching weed seeds, which triggers germination. Even if they do germinate, they run out of food before they reach the light – so they shrivel and die.

When the seedlings have filled out and formed tiny plants, transplant some to create the right final spacing, as described before. When they reach about 30cm (12in) tall, give them support.

Spring or autumn sowing?

I sow three-quarters of my hardy annuals in the autumn in preference to the spring. I've found there are several advantages to autumn sowing. You get bigger plants; they live and flower longer and they steam ahead like a train when conditions improve the following spring. Autumn-sown seeds form small plants before winter,

53

(Below) A patch of mixed sunflowers including *Helianthus annuus* 'Valentine'.

(Opposite) I love the satin texture of the black peony poppy. Cut the seed pods in half and float them too.

which then go into a semi-hibernation that is induced by decreasing light intensity, day length and temperature. Above soil level, growth stops, but below, root growth continues. Over the winter, a large root ball develops unseen. As light and warmth increase again in spring, the plant romps away. It has a huge root system to nourish a fast-growing, bumper plant.

A spring-sown seed has rather pathetic prospects in comparison. Spring conditions are perfect for top and root growth to develop at the same time, so the plant doesn't develop the huge root reserves to support a giant plant. Spring-sown plants do fine, but are seldom as productive as flower factories as the autumn-sown ones. Autumn sowing is like getting money in the bank without much sweat – the cutting patch will be already half-full, and will be bursting at the seams the following year.

If you sow in the autumn, you'll avoid expanses of empty, fallow ground, characteristic of the average winter plot. With hardy annuals in place, you'll have different colors and textures of foliage to look at through the winter. My favourites are the California poppies (*Eschscholzia californica*) with their elegant, silvery, finely cut foliage – wonderful covered in frost and dew. I sow lots of these to line paths and borders. They don't die down and disappear, but look bright and healthy in the leanest times.

Early autumn is a relatively quiet time in the garden. You'll have lots of harvesting to do, picking flowers and vegetables, and there will still be some weeding, but most of the chores – watering, staking and mowing – are coming to an end. Compare this to the frantic rush of spring and early summer, when there are lots of vegetables to plant and sow and all the half-hardy annuals to be raised and cared for.

Most autumn-sown plants will be in bloom by the middle of May, and a few, such as cerinthe, California poppies and marigolds, six weeks earlier than that. Your garden will be full of flowers to fill the early summer gap, when spring-flowering bulbs are over and the spring-sown annuals, perennials and roses haven't gotten going.

Plants that are best sown in spring

I know from experience that these softies don't survive the winter on my heavy clay, especially if the winter is wet.
dill (*Anethum*)
grasses
red orache (*Atriplex*)
sunflowers (*Helianthus*)

Spring or autumn

Depending on climate, sow these in spring or autumn.
annual clary (*Salvia viridis*)
honeywort (*Cerinthe*)
larkspur (*Consolida*)
pot marigolds (*Calendula*)

Autumn-sown survivors

These survive on my heavy clay whatever the autumn and winter weather. They are the hardiest: choose them if you garden in cold areas, at high altitudes, or in an exposed site.
Ammi majus
Bupleurum rotundifolium
cornflowers (*Centaurea*)
California poppies (*Eschscholzia*)
love-in-a-mist (*Nigella*)
poppies (*Papaver*), most species and cultivars
scabious (*Scabiosa*)
violas, most species and cultivars

I'm lucky enough to garden in a fairly mild climate compared to gardeners in the north, where the winters can be a lot colder. If you do live in a very frost-prone region, you can sow an autumn crop under cloches or homemade fleece mini-tunnels, which should give just enough added protection from frost and excessive wet. Good drainage and soils that are not too high in nitrogen (which promotes soft growth) will also aid survival. Having said that, many hardy annuals are tougher than they're given credit for and, if you're an adventurous gardener, you might take the risk and learn something that books don't tell you.

Foliage and upper-story annuals

Some of the best foliage plants you can grow are hardy annuals. Grow plenty of basic (primary) foliage plants such as *Euphorbia oblongata*, along with some fillers and upper-story plants too.

Ammi majus,
Bishop's flower

1.2m (4ft)
Climate zones 4–7

Description
A lovely cow parsley-like plant, but more delicate and longer lasting, both as a cut flower and in the garden. It doesn't have that characteristic cow parsley smell either. Strip most of the leaves before arranging – they die more quickly than the flowers.

Role
Totally invaluable foliage filler for those that like country-style arrangements, and superb on its own in a large glass vase. Dramatic and stylish as a hanging globe (see page 49).

Good combinations
Lovely with other whites and greens and mixed with blues. Use it as a base and dot *Consolida ajacis* 'Blue Cloud' all through.

Special growing requirements
Easy germination and cultivation. Best thinned to 45cm (18in) apart to give individual plants enough room. If sown in autumn they will reach 1.2m (4ft). If sown in spring they will be a bit shorter. Needs netting support.

Anethum graveolens,
Dill

90cm (3ft)
Climate zones 3–7

Description
Brilliant acid green plateau of light, airy flowers, like fennel, but green, not gold. The florists' selection has bigger flowers and smaller leaves than the usual herb variety.

Role
Wonderful filler foliage.

Good combinations
Superb with bright, strong colors and good with whites and blues. I love this with sunflower, *Helianthus* 'Deep Red' (see page 45).

Special growing requirements
Germinates best and self-seeds in poor, well-drained soils. On heavy clay, I add grit to the sowing position. Does not like root disturbance, so best sown where it is to flower. Doesn't survive the winter with me, so sow in the spring. Thin to 25–30cm (10–12in). Needs netting support.

Atriplex hortensis var. *rubra*, Red orache

1.5m (5ft)
Climate zones 8–11 (winter planted), later spring in northern zones

Description
Fleshy, crimson-leaved plant that forms a substantial bush. In late summer, it's covered in coin-like seed cases, very elegant and rich.

Role
One of the most versatile plants in the cutting garden. Pick large stems for primary or filler foliage, and use seed pods, formed in late summer, as an upper story. This plant is edible too. Pick small side buds for a mixed leaf salad and steam larger leaves, as you would spinach.

Good combinations
Lovely used as the filler foliage with euphorbia, with orange Iceland poppies and alliums, but good with almost anything (see page 139).

Special growing requirements
Won't survive the winter on a heavy soil, so sow in spring. Self-seeds prolifically. Pinch out the tips when 30cm (12in) tall, to encourage bushing out. Thin and space to at least 45cm (18in) apart. In spring arrangements, sear stem ends of new growth in boiling water. Needs individual support.

Briza maxima,
Greater quaking grass

45cm (18in)
Climate zone 5

Description
A beautiful grass with tall stems, hung with flowers that look like raindrops as they catch the light.

Role
One of the best upper story plants you can grow – delicate and dramatic at the same time. I also love this on its own in a Moroccan tea glass, for putting beside a bed.

Good combinations
Use it with any combination, in a hand-tied bunch or a small vase. Add five or seven stems as you finish the arrangement for an instantly elegant silhouette.

Special growing requirements
Easy germination and will self-seed. Lovely self-sown through gravel paths and terraces. Thin to 25–30cm (10–12in). Dries well, hung upside down and tied with a rubber band.

Bupleurum rotundifolium

60cm (2ft)
Climate zones 7–9

Description
Similar to a euphorbia in color and flower structure, but doesn't have the allergenic, milky sap.

Role
An excellent foliage filler. Not substantial enough to use as primary foliage.

Good combinations
Good with calm whites and blues, as well as the rich Venetian colors.

Special growing requirements
Germinates best and self-seeds in poor, well-drained soils. On heavy clay, I add grit to the sowing position. Needs pinching out. Does not like root disturbance, so best sown where it is to flower. Thin to 25–30cm (10–12in). Needs netting support.

Cerinthe major 'Purpurascens', Honeywort
45cm (18in)
Climate zones 7–9

Description
Silver leaves contrast to purple, bell-shaped flowers. Invaluable for flowering from early spring. I make several sowings of this and transplant self-sown seedlings into the cutting patch. The species, *Cerinthe major*, is also lovely, with a bold yellow stripe on the purple flowers.

Role
Excellent as filler foliage and an upper story.

Good combinations
Can be mixed with anything in the garden and the vase. It looks wonderful with the green-flowered *Zinnia elegans* 'Envy'.

Special growing requirements
Tough-coated seed; it's best soaked overnight before sowing. It does well in poor soil, where it will flower more prolifically than in rich, fertile loam. On heavy clay, I add grit to the planting position. Needs warmth for quick germination, so I often sow in pots inside. Will self-sow and seedlings should survive the winter. Thin to 25–30cm (10–12in). Sear stem ends in boiling water.

Euphorbia oblongata
60cm (2ft)
Climate zones 8–11

Description
The most productive, bright acid-green plant, which I pick more than any other. And it's in flower by mid February. It is in fact a short-lived perennial, but I pick from it so heavily, it gets exhausted and is best sown every autumn. You'll want it in huge quantities, so line it up instead of box (*Buxus*) around the edge of your beds.

Role
The best basic foliage plant there is, creating an interesting skeleton for any medium-sized arrangement. Wear gloves to protect yourself from the allergenic milky sap.

Good combinations
Wonderful contrast to bright, strong colors and equally good with pale and pastel colors.

Special growing requirements
None, very tolerant. Will even grow in shade. It is slower than others to germinate, so if you can, sow it under cover for quicker flowers. Will self-sow. Space plants at 45cm (18in). Sear stem ends in boiling water.

Hordeum jubatum, Squirrel tail grass
45cm (18in)
Climate zone 5

Description
Looks like an ornamental barley with long, whiskered plumes. A superb, light airy plant for threading through from the front to the back of the border.

Role
Lovely as an upper story, or used as a filler.

Good combinations
I use this in a corn-stook type arrangement with lots of grasses, cornflowers, marigolds and poppies.

Special growing requirements
Does not like root disturbance, so best sown where it is to flower. Doesn't survive the winter with me, so sow in the spring. Thin to 25–30cm (10–12in). Dries well, hung upside down and fastened with a rubber band.

Panicum miliaceum 'Violaceum'
60cm (2ft)
Climate zones 4–9

Description
This is one of my favorite grasses; it's green, with a lovely wash of crimson at the tips.

Role
Lovely upper story plant. Cascades with great elegance in the garden and the vase.

Good combinations
Goes with any color, strong or pale.

Special growing requirements
Does not like root disturbance, so best sown where it is to flower. Doesn't survive the winter with me, so sow in the spring. Self-sows. Thin to 25–30cm (10–12in). Dries well, hung upside down and tied with a rubber band.

Papaver somniferum, Opium poppy
1.2m (4ft)
Climate zones 2–7

Description
Elegant, silvery, indented leaves and huge poppy flowers. 'The Giant' is bright pink and there is also a lovely frilly, almost black one, *P. somniferum* var. *paeoniflorum* 'Black Peony' (see page 55).

Role
The flowers won't last in a vase whatever you do to them, so pick the seed pods and use them as an upper story. Floated petals won't drop for 24 hours.

Good combinations
Silvery-green, pepper-pot seedpods go well with anything. Cut them in half and float them in a shallow bowl (see page 55).

Special growing requirements
Very easy in a soil with a fine tilth. They don't like root disturbance, so if you want to transplant seedlings, do so when they're still tiny. Self-sows. Thin to 25–30cm (10–12in). Will dry well if hung upside down and tied with a rubber band.

Salvia viridis 'Oxford Blue' and 'Pink Sundae', Annual clary
45cm (18in)
All zones

Description
A hardy salvia, in which the flowers are minute, but the flower bracts are enlarged and brilliantly colored. This is an exceptionally long-flowering annual, looking good if you keep picking it from June to September. Use it like lavender, lining your paths. I lined the sweet pea tunnel with the blue this year.

Role
Use as a filler or upper story foliage.

Good combinations
The brilliant blue form is fantastic with acid-green, orange marigolds and poppies. I use the pink with acid-green and sky-blue or magenta.

Special growing requirements
Easy germination and cultivation. Thin to 25–30cm (10–12in). Will dry well if hung upside down and tied with a rubber band.

My favorite hardy annual flowers

All these flowers are very easy to grow and you don't need any special gardening para- phernalia to do so. Get going with just a packet of seed, some empty soil, a spade and a rake. It's all you need to fill your house with endless flowers.

Calendula officinalis 'Indian Prince', English or Pot marigold
45cm (18in)
All zones

Description
C. officinalis 'Indian Prince' is my favorite marigold, a sophisticated flower with deep orange petals, that contrast with the rich, dark crimson buds, centers and petal reverses. You can also grow a color mix, 'Touch of Red', in apricots, yellows and oranges, all with crimson petal backs.

Role
A perfect bridesmaid for a large vase, or arrange it on its own in turquoise or a Moroccan glass (see page 53).

Good combinations
Use with the lily-flowered tulips 'Ballerina' and 'Mariette' in spring, and with orange Iceland poppies and *Anchusa* in summer.

Special growing requirements
Very easy. It will germinate and grow well in any position in full sun. Will get mildew as they tire at the end of a dry season. The quickest flower from seed to bloom – 8 weeks from a mid-spring sowing. From an autumn sowing, will be in flower by early May. Thin to 25–30cm (10–12in).

Centaurea cyanus 'Black Ball', Cornflower
90cm (3ft)
Climate zones 7–10

Description
Rich crimson-black cornflower that way out-does the blue variety 'Blue Boy' as a cut flower and garden plant. The flowers do not bleach as in the blue and it has a long vase life of about 7 days.

Role
One of the best bridesmaids you can grow.

Good combinations
Arrange the black with *Allium hollandicum* 'Purple Sensation' and *Papaver nudicaule* 'Red Sail', or use it in a tied bunch with *Lysimachia atropurpurea* 'Beaujolais'.

Special growing requirements
Very easy. Grows slightly shorter from a spring sowing – 60cm (2ft). Thin to 25–30cm (10–12in). Needs netting support.

Centaurea cyanus 'Red Boy', Cornflower

90cm (3ft)
Climate zones 7–10

Description
A deep, magenta-pink cornflowers which came second in my trials of cornflowers at home. The flowers don't bleach and they have a vase life of 5–7 days and a garden life of 8–10 weeks.

Role
These are wonderful in simple arrangements with calendulas and make good bridesmaids to similar deep pink colored flowers.

Good combinations
Use them with magenta sweet William (*Dianthus barbatus* 'Oschberg'), the magenta *Gladiolus communis* subsp. *byzantinus* and bright pink and magenta roses.

Special growing requirements
Very easy to grow. It's best from an autumn sowing as you get bumper-sized plants which produce buckets and buckets of cut flowers.

Consolida ajacis 'Deep Blue', Larkspur

60–90cm (2–3ft)
All zones

Description
Deep, purple-blue spikes with double flowers all the way up the stem. There is also a good pure white, single color form.

Role
Use as bride, or gatecrasher in a large glass vase. Dries well. Lie flat in a warm, dark dry place, such as the airing cupboard.

Good combinations
The blue works with every color – strong or pale. Use the white with bright greens and blues.

Special growing requirements
Larkspurs can be difficult to germinate. Put the packet of seed in the freezer for a week before you sow. Doesn't like root disturbance so it's best direct-sown. May not overwinter in cold, wet winters. Thin to 25–30cm (10–12in). Needs netting support.

Consolida regalis 'Blue Cloud', Larkspur

60–90cm (2–3ft)
All zones

Description
A delicate, small-flowered cultivar of larkspur in brilliant blue. The flowers are arranged on long, individual stems, forming a cloud, rather than a vertical spire.

Role
Lovely as a flower-foliage base for a medium-sized arrangement.

Good combinations
Poke in white Iceland poppies, *Ammi majus*, or *Calendula officinalis* 'Indian Prince'.

Special growing requirements
Larkspurs can be difficult to germinate. Put the packet of seed in the freezer for a week before you sow. May not overwinter in cold, wet conditions. Thin to 25–30cm (10–12in). Needs netting support

(Opposite)
Red orache (*Atriplex hortensis*) and dill (*Anethum graveolens*).

58

Eschscholzia californica 'Orange King', California poppy
30cm (12in)
Climate zones 9–10

Description
The best hardy annual for lining paths and terraces. Beautiful silver leaves and trumpet-shaped tangerine flowers.

Role
Short-lived once cut and the flowers shut up at night, so best arranged on their own in a simple glass.

Good combinations
This orange is lovely with blue cornflowers (*Centaurea cyanus*) and *Nigella damascena*. I have this combination lining the main path in the cutting garden and mix them in a vase.

Special growing requirements
Very easy in any soil. Self-sows. Thin to 25–30cm (10–12in).

Helianthus annuus 'Deep Red', Sunflower

2–2.5m (6–8ft)
Climate zones 4–9

Description
Glamorous, velvety flowers in deep, rich crimson. One of the most sumptuous flowers in the autumn garden.

Role
Arrange it on its own, or with other statuesque flowers.

Good combinations
Mix this in a large vase with acid-green euphorbia, using the half-hardy *Rudbeckia* 'Rustic Colors' as the bridesmaid. The two match perfectly in color and texture. Also lovely with dill (*Anethum graveolens*) (see page 56).

Special growing requirements
Very easy. Must be sown in the spring, not autumn. Seed of florist's sunflowers are expensive, so don't waste them. Sow two seeds, 5cm (2in) apart at 45cm (18in) spacings. From these two, one is bound to germinate. If they both do, transplant one somewhere else. Pinch out the tips when the seedlings reach 15–18cm (6–8 in) tall. Needs individual staking. Grows to 3m (10ft) if pinched out.

Helianthus annuus 'Valentine', Sunflower

2–2.5m (6–8ft)
Climate zones 2–11

Description
This is my favorite yellow sunflower – pale lemon yellow, rather than golden, Van Gogh yellow. Lovely chocolate centers and the right-sized flowers – not too big, not too small – on long, straight stems.

Role
Arrange it on its own, or with other statuesque flowers.

Good combinations
Mix it with artichokes in bloom, amaranthus and large-flowered dahlias, such as 'Rip City'.

Special growing requirements
Grow this as for *H. annuus* 'Deep Red'. Pinching out is not so crucial for this type. It will only reach 2–2.3m (6–7ft) if left to its own devices. Pinched out, they do bush out more and you get an increased number of smaller blooms on the end of strong, straight stems. Needs individual staking.

Helianthus debilis subsp. *cucumerifolius* 'Vanilla Ice'
90cm–1.2m (3–4ft)
Climate zones 8–11

Description
This sunflower has smaller flowers and much thinner stems than *H. annuus*. The flowers are the color of vanilla ice cream. There is also a golden-yellow form called 'Pan' (see page 23).

Role
Pretty on its own, or in a mixed bunch or vase. Perfect for mixed bunches and ideal size for children to pick.

Good combinations
Lovely with *Cosmos bipinnatus* 'Purity' and Bells of Ireland, *Moluccella laevis*. 'Pan' is good with crimson dahlias, amaranthus and *Scabiosa atropurpurea* 'Ace of Spades'.

Special growing requirements
As for *H. annuus* 'Valentine', sow at 45cm (18in) spacings. Needs individual staking.

Lychnis coronaria Oculata Group, Ruby flax
60cm (2ft)
Climate zones 3–8

Description
The most delicate flower I grow for cutting. It has fine, sheeny, deep magenta-pink flowers and it blooms for many months at a stretch.

Role
Pick it for a simple bedside table arrangement.

Good combinations
I love this with seedpods, such as those of *Nigella hispanica* and opium poppy (*Papaver somniferum*).

Special growing requirements
Very easy, robust and quick growing. It looks good for a long time too. Thin to 30cm (12in).

Lupinus 'Blue Spear'

90cm (3ft)
Climate zones 2–6

Description
Beautiful bright Moroccan-blue flowers, the spikes topped with a brush of yellow and white over the hood of the flower. Further down the stem, the hoods are purple and crimson. The foliage is handsome too, like a finer, thinner version of a cannabis leaf.

Role
This is one of the most elegant plants I grow for arranging, one stem on its own, in a tall, narrow bottle. It has fine flowers and a wonderful shape with a twist and turn to every stem.

Good combinations
It also makes the perfect bride to the blue cornflower bridesmaid and is useful as an upper story flower to be added right at the end of a large vase arrangement.

Special growing requirements
Easy to grow, doing best in a freely drained soil with lots of organic material dug in. It can get mildew on the foilage in a dry year.

Malope trifida 'Vulcan', Annual mallow

90cm (3ft)
Climate zones 7–10

Description
Beautiful, magenta flowers with a rich satin texture to the petals. A startling, bright-green eye in the center of the flower. The buds are a good Chinese-lantern shape.

Role
Excellent for large arrangements, forming the foliage base, gatecrasher, or bridesmaid.

Good combinations
I love this color with orange, blue and green and with other magentas and crimsons (see page 22).

Special growing requirements
Very easy, robust and quick growing. It looks good for a long time too. Thin to 45cm (18in).

Nigella damascena 'Deep Blue' & 'Double White', Love-in-a-mist
60cm (2ft)
All zones

Description
Wonderful mid-blue or white flowers with elegant green whiskers all the way round. The best green, cheesy, football seedpods. The white form looks like a Tudor ruff.

Role
Use the flowers as bridesmaids and the seedpods as foliage fillers or the perfect upper story.

Good combinations
Arrange it with anything.

Special growing requirements
Very easy. Self-sows prolifically. Best direct sown – they hate root disturbance. You must thin the seedlings rather than just leaving where they are. Be brave and brutal, thin to 20–30cm (8–12in) apart.

Nigella hispanica, Love-in-a-mist

60cm (2ft)
All zones

Description
This nigella has larger flowers, in a deeper blue than the more common *N. damascena*. It has rich crimson stamens too. Rather than green, football seed cases, it develops spectacular crimson crowns (see pages 46–7).

Role
One of the best bridesmaids you can grow.

Good combinations
Arrange with orange, or in a classic combination of blue, white and acid-green and use the seedpods as an upper story (see page 45).

Special growing requirements
More difficult to germinate than *N. damascena*. It likes more heat and a freely drained soil, so sow it early in the autumn and late in the spring. Thin to 25–30cm (10–12in).

Papaver rhoeas Shirley Series Mixed, Corn poppy
90cm (3ft)
All zones

Description
Looks ethereal and delicate, lovely in the garden and in a vase. Flowers in pink, white, silver, red and mauve.

Role
Arrange them on their own in a glass vase for the kitchen table.

Good combinations
These are best not mixed with other things, as they don't last as long as other cut flowers.

Special growing requirements
Very easy. Will self-sow. Thin to 25–30cm (10–12in). The petals won't stay on the flowers for a minute if you don't sear the stem ends.

Scabiosa atropurpurea, Pincushion flower
60–90cm (2–3ft)
All zones

Description
Soft, pompon flowers in white, mauve, pink, crimson and bright red. Very long-lasting cut flowers and will pump out blooms from June until December in a sheltered spot. There is a sensational velvety dark crimson-black cultivar, 'Black Cat'.

Role
Lovely on its own, all colors mixed up together, or pick each color separately and use them as bridesmaids or gatecrashers in mixed arrangements.

Good combinations
'Black Cat' is wonderful with *Dahlia* 'Black Fire' or 'Rip City', in contrast with velvety *Tithonia* and green amaranthus. It also looks good in contrast to malope (see page 42).

Special growing requirements
As a short-lived perennial, this takes longer to germinate and grow than other hardy annuals. Sow it early under cover with half-hardy annuals, but it's frost-hardy so you can plant it out in autumn, or in mid-spring, before the last frosts. Thin to 25–30cm (10–12in). Needs netting support.

Viola 'Deep Purple'

8–10cm (3–4in)
All zones

Description
A large flowered pansy with deep purple flowers. One of the richest textured petals you can pick. I also grow the deep mahogany-crimson 'Ruby'.

Role
Invaluable for February, March and April picking when there is little else around. I grow them in pots down the side of the main path in the garden and pick them regularly to arrange in small glasses and egg cups, scattered around the house.

Good combinations
Lovely with gold and orange crocus and other small spring bulbs. Combine them together in small, colored glasses, or a turquoise bowl.

Special growing requirements
Sow them under cover in early autumn. Plant them into pots by the middle of October for flowering sporadically through the winter and more prolifically in late winter and early spring.

sweet peas

❁ Sweet peas are hardy annuals, but there are so many of them and they're so good as cut flowers, that they deserve a section of their own. They are the best climbers for the cutting patch, giving you arches, teepees and tunnels to bring a vertical dimension into the garden. ❁

The strongest scents

Sweet peas have one of the most extraordinary scents in the world. There's no point growing sweet peas that don't smell. Pushing your nose into one of them would be like biting into a dry orange, all pith and no juice; or an Easter egg, beautifully wrapped and ribboned, but made of the cheapest chocolate. Take the scent away from a sweet pea and, as far as I'm concerned, you're better off growing something else.

I don't mind how many flowers there are on a sweet pea stem. Nor how big the flowers are. In fact, I almost prefer the small, straight-edged kinds, rather than the ones that are ruffled like a ballerina's tutu. Long stems are good, but short stems aren't the end of the world. Modern breeding programs have concentrated on producing multi-headed, Goliath sweet peas with stems that reach nearly 45cm (18in) long. I've got enough large, long-stemmed, multi-headed, glamorous flowers in my cutting patch and don't need any more. What I

want is scent – sweet, heady and all-enveloping – and that is what's difficult to find.

With many new cultivars of sweet pea I've tried (even those that are sold as highly scented) the fragrance, if there is any at all, is so faint as to be almost completely absent. With these, there's no chance of the perfume wafting towards you and filling a room. No chance of having a bunch by your bed, so that the first thing that hits you in the morning is that unique and unmistakable sweetness.

Old-fashioned stock

To get reliably, sweetly scented sweet peas, you have to be a Luddite and return to the so-called 'Old-fashioned' sweet peas, or at least the new ones directly bred from that gene pool. Return to 17th-century Italy, or to 18th- and 19th-century Britain and you'll be fine. I have teepees of 'Matucana' and the identical 'Cupani's Original' all round my garden. They're the strongest scented sweet peas you can grow and are a wonderful color, rich crimson wings and a purple snout.

'Cupani' was first cultivated in a monastery at Palermo in Sicily by a monk in 1699. He discovered a highly scented wild flower and brought it into cultivation in the monastery garden. He improved the stock, and it grew higher and its flowers larger than those of the original plant in the wild. Father Cupani sent seed to Britain, and it became the parent of all the other sweet peas we know. He also sent seed to Peru, where it was grown in the Andean village of Matucana. Offspring of this arrived in Britain much later, in the 19th century, virtually the same plant as 'Cupani', but with a different horticultural history.

There are other cultivars whose perfume is almost as strong as the famous two. 'Painted Lady' is the runner-up on a blindfold test. This was first introduced into London's Chelsea Physic Garden in 1737. It has a lovely pink snout, with paler pink wings. And there's the rich, dark crimson 'Black Knight' (1898) which comes close behind.

(Opposite) The pink *Lathyrus odoratus* 'Matucana'. The strongest scented sweet pea you can grow.

(Below) The painted frame of sweet pea 'Painted Lady' fills this corner of the garden with its unmistakable scent.

I have all three of the above growing on a hazel stick tunnel. This is home-made, using hazel poles pushed into the ground down both sides of the path, with thinner sticks bent in a hoop between the two sides and tied with a bit of wire and twine. Wood freshly cut in January or February will be more pliable.

A teepee made from bamboo canes or hazel wands is equally easy to create. Push a circle of eight poles into the ground, sinking them 20–30cm (8–12in) deep. The circle should be about 1m (3ft) across. Gather the eight uprights together with a piece of wire or twine at the top. If you use canes, or your branches aren't twiggy enough to make a real witches' broom, add smaller sticks, or circles of string at the base. You need these to give the plants enough handholds to attach themselves to and climb. All sweet peas can grow to 2.5–3m (8–10ft) depending how you train them.

When to sow sweet peas

I sow my sweet peas in the autumn and you can too, even if you grow in colder winter climates than mine. You'll get larger plants from an autumn sowing than if you sow them in spring. They'll flower earlier too. I start picking mine in the second or third week of May. It would be at least a month later if I'd sown them in spring. Early summer (late May and early June) can be lean times, so the more plants you can encourage to flower then, the better.

When I sowed sweet peas in the spring, they often suffered from mildew at the base as they got tired after a month or so of flowering. This is particularly true in a hot summer. Sown in the autumn, they seem better able to resist this disease, probably because they're more robust, with a more extensive root system. What's more, sown then, you'll have one less thing to do next spring.

(Below) A bowl of sweet peas. Mix strong colors like bright pink 'Janet Scott' with green *Lathyrus chloranthus*.

(Opposite) I made several candelabra like this for a ruby wedding party (see p144).

How to grow sweet peas

1 Sow any time in the autumn, with two seeds to a small pot. I usually use root trainers – long, thin plastic pots – for my sweet peas. All legumes, these included, dislike root disturbance and thrive best with a deep root run, so deep pots like these are ideal. Cardboard toilet-paper rolls are a cheap alternative. I use multi-purpose compost. Dampen the compost surface and then push each seed in, about 2.5cm (1in) deep, with your finger. I never bother to soak the seeds. Some people do this overnight, to soften the hard coat, but I tend to forget them and they ferment and then rot. They'll germinate without soaking within 1–2 weeks.

2 Cover the pots with an empty compost bag, sheets of newspaper, or a polystyrene tile to keep moisture and warmth in and light out. A little extra warmth will speed germination, but is not essential.

3 It's important to set a mousetrap near your sweet peas. Mice love the seed and your whole crop may disappear in one go.

4 Check for germination every day. Once the seedlings appear, keep them cool at about 5°C (41°F). This promotes root growth rather than rapid stem growth, which is exactly what you want. A cold greenhouse or cold frame is ideal, but your plants will be fine in a light potting shed, stored on a window ledge.

5 Pinch out the leader – the growing tip – when there are three or four pairs of leaves. Just squeeze it off between your finger and thumb, reducing the plant to 5cm (2in) in height. This promotes vigorous sideshoot formation because the energy of the plant goes into forming flowering stems, growing out, not up.

6 Every three to four weeks, go and check your plants. Keep them watered (just moist, not sodden) and pinch out any spindly tips, if they have started to shoot again.

7 Check the bottom of the pot for white roots. If there are any visible through the holes in the bottom, pot the plants up. I put the two seedlings from one root trainer into a 2-liter (3½-pint) herbaceous perennial pot. Two seedlings spaced 5cm (2in) apart are the perfect

(Opposite) **My most highly-scented bunch. Black sweet Williams, sweet peas and perennial stock (see p144).**

(Below) *Lathyrus odoratus* **'Janet Scott' and** *L. chloranthus* **on a couple of peastick wigwams.**

covering for one vertical upright. Water them in. You'll only need to cover the cold frame if exceptionally hard frosts are forecast.

8 By early spring (March) you can plant them out. By now, roots will have filled a 2-liter (3½-pint) pot. Pick a spell of mild weather to plant them out in the garden. Place them 5–8cm (2–3in) away from the support – a teepee, an arch, or a tunnel. Surround them with slug prevention. I use at least a 30cm (1ft) wide strip of horticultural sharp sand, 5cm (2in) deep, all round mine.

9 As the young plants begin to grow, tie them into the frame with soft string; don't leave them to flop around. They'll grow more quickly and make stronger plants if tied in regularly; every two weeks for the first month, and then more often when they start to romp away. Professional and serious amateur growers, who are going to compete in horticultural shows, will tell you to pinch out all the curly tendrils. They take energy from the flowers, and attach themselves to flower stems and bend them into curves. It's a lot of work on the scale of a tunnel. I try to remove any I see while I pick, but I don't get bogged down.

10 Then just let them get on with it and pick, pick, pick. If you see any seed pods as you're cutting, snip these off. You don't want your plants forming seed or it will stop the plants producing flowers. When the flowers are coming to an end, you can collect some seeds for sowing next year. If you have grown several different kinds, they may have cross-pollinated and you'll end up with a mixed bag, but they should all have good scent.

Cordon sweet peas

If you want sweet peas with long stems that are perfectly straight with lots of large flowers on one stem, it's a good idea to grow them on the cordon system. This involves lots of work and I tend to have too many other things to do to grow my sweet peas in this way, but if you have time, give it a go. You get a neat line of plants, rather than a jumble of stems. There will also be fewer flower stems, but each one is a bumper-size.

When you plant them out in early spring, remove all but one or two stems growing from the base. Go for two if you've got a couple of strong, thick stems. Otherwise just select and keep one.

As they grow, you must continue to pinch out all side branches and tendrils as they form. The energy then goes into one momentous stem, which will develop into something the width of a finger, rather than bushing out into several. Tie this stem regularly into a cane.

Once the single or double stems have reached the tops of their canes, untie them and run them along the ground, then reattach them two or three canes further along the row. Then train them up that cane. Pinch out the tips again if they reach the top of the second cane. When they start to flower, you can start to pick.

The best sweet peas

You have to grow some sweet peas to pick. They flower very early and productive, giving you up to ten bunches a week from one teepee. In arrangements, *Alchemilla mollis* is a traditional partner of sweet peas, but why not try the green-flowered pea, *Lathyrus chloranthus*, instead?

Sweet peas can be grown as annuals in all climate zones.

Lathyrus chloranthus

Description
This is a species, rather than a hybrid, with lime-green flowers. The blooms are small and not scented. *L. chloranthus* is not a strong grower, taking 4–6 weeks to germinate and twice as long to flower as other sweet peas, but they're worth it. Because they are slow, you're best to sow these in the autumn or late winter.

Good combinations
Excellent as contrast in color to other varieties of sweet pea. Use these as gate-crashers in any sweet pea bunch. They look marvellous in a bunch with any of the dark, rich colors; 'Cupani', 'Janet Scott' (see page 66) and 'Black Knight', as well as with white or cream.

Lathyrus odoratus 'Black Knight'

Description
First bred in 1898, it is a deep crimson, almost black variety of sweet pea. 8/10 for scent.

Good combinations
Pick this with 'Gipsy Queen' and arrange them in a turquoise jug. Collect a series of three down the centre of your table. Children love arranging these.

Lathyrus odoratus 'Gipsy Queen'

Description
A 1950s cultivar, with larger blooms than the rest and you'll see a suggestion of the wavy edged petals that many modern cultivars are bred with. It does not have a very powerful scent, (7/10) but I love its rich, ruby red flowers.

Good combinations
At its best with all the other rich, deep colors.

Lathyrus odoratus 'Janet Scott'

Description
The best deep pink I've grown.

Good combinations
Lovely with just green, the flowers floating in a shallow glass plate (see page 66).

Lathyrus odoratus 'Lord Nelson'

Description
First bred in 1907.The best deep purplish navy blue. 8/10 for scent.

Good combinations
I love to use this with mauve, (see page 62) or with cream.

Lathyrus odoratus 'Matucana'

Description
Another of my favorites, very similar to 'Cupani' with extraordinary scent and intense purple and crimson, bicolored flowers. 10/10 for scent.

Good combinations
One of the best for arranging on its own, or mixed in with the other dark colors, with a splash of green.

Lathyrus odoratus 'Mrs Collier'

Description
Another old cultivar. This is the best cream, with strong scent (8/10). Many of the whites and creams have a brownish tinge to the snouts, which makes them look half dead as soon as they flower. Not with this one. It's just a pure, bright cream.

Good combinations
Good as contrast to many of the other colors.

Lathyrus odoratus 'Painted Lady'

Description
First bred in 1737, it is the best pale pink, with mid-pink wings and a paler snout. 9/10 for scent.

Good combinations
Combine this with cream 'Mrs Collier' in a blue tea glass.

**(Opposite)
My homemade sweet pea tunnel. I mix all colors together in a random jamboree.**

biennials

 Biennials are plants that form roots and leaves in the first year, but only flower, set seed and die in the second. Like annuals, they are cut-and-come-again flowers. The more you pick, the more they flower.

Invaluable additions

Biennials aren't grown nearly enough. It's easy to be put off by the hassle of sowing seed and then having to wait a year before seeing any flowers. People tell me over and over again: biennials are boring because you don't get instant results. They leave a blank space in the garden for several months and then, like annuals, they're only short-lived, so you've got to start the whole process again.

Don't be discouraged though. Biennials include some of the best cutting plants you can get. They don't leave blank spaces – biennials have foliage above ground all winter. If you cut them frequently, they also have a long flowering season, many of them way outdoing perennials for the number of months they take center stage until they collapse, exhausted, towards the end of summer. And, like perennials, they possess a scale and stature that give a garden a feeling of maturity within a year. If you've got a brand new garden,

a newly created border, or a patch devoted to cut flowers, and you feel the lack of substance and the decent-sized verticals needed for a balanced design, then go for biennials. The garden will soon look like it has been there for years.

Perpetual and prolific

That's not all. Most biennials self-sow, but not so promiscuously that you curse the moment you introduced them. I've banned forget-me-nots from my garden for this reason. Some years, I've weeded out more forget-me-not than chickweed, but you don't have to worry about this with the ones I recommend. There will be a scattering of offspring all around the parent

(Below) The cutting garden in June full of biennials: here *Onopordum acanthium* makes a robust and statuesque windbreak – and you can pick it too.
(Opposite) Tied bunch of biennials (see p144).

(Below) Cardoon leaves mixed with honesty make a generous, billowing base for spring tulips (see p144).

plant, but not willy-nilly all over the garden. You can leave the seedlings where they are, thinning them out to give them enough room to thrive, or you can transplant them to another place (see opposite).

They're invaluable in their season of flowering too. In both the cutting garden and ornamental garden, the turn of the season between spring and summer can be a momentary blip in the color bonanza. Tulips are over and the bulk of annuals haven't yet gotten going. Biennials, along with autumn-sown hardy annuals, plug this gap, flowering prolifically from the middle of May. The demonstration gardens at the Chelsea Flower Show are always stacked with biennials – they can be guaranteed to flower in that crucial third week of May.

Which biennials to grow

My favorite biennial is the Iceland poppy (*Papaver nudicaule* 'Meadow Pastels'). No one should be without

this plant. It's the best cut flower on my whole seed list. If you sear the stems in boiling water for thirty seconds, it lasts a week in water. You can pick it in full flower, or in tight bud and it will open as it stands in the vase. But don't just think of it as a cut flower. I love it in the rest of the garden too. By early May it's covered in huge, saucer-sized blooms, with ten to fifteen flowers on each plant. They're like crumpled swatches of fine silk, a palmful on the end of each stem. I love the colors in this mix – pink, white, cream, primrose and orange – bright and pale together; and each is scented like a Tazetta narcissus. If you don't want mixed colors, go for *P. nudicaule* 'Red Sail', which is just as good – a single color, the red-orange of tomato soup, but without the scent. Drifts of both these plants look good in late spring and they'll still be looking good in late summer if you keep picking the flowers – live- rather than dead-heading, not allowing them to run to seed.

How to grow biennials

Biennials should be sown any time between the middle of May and the middle of July. Most can be sown straight into the ground, as for hardy annuals (see page 48). There are a few, such as the Iceland poppy (*Papaver nudicaule*) that are best sown with more care under cover (see below).

If you sow biennials earlier than May, they will try to flower the first year. You can manipulate this to your advantage with Iceland poppies. Sown in March with half-hardy annuals, *Papaver nudicaule* cultivars will flower in August and September, but plants that flower in their first year will not flower again, so you need to sow in early summer as well for next season's crop.

If you sow biennials later than mid-July, they won't make large enough plants to survive the winter outside. You'll have to overwinter them under cover, and plant them out in early spring and they never make such productive plants.

Sowing straight into the ground

Most biennials are very happy when sown straight into the ground. The best way to do this is select a small plot to use as a nursery bed.

Make sure the ground is weed free and work the soil to a fine tilth (see page 48). Then sow the seed as thinly as you can in rows that are 15–30cm (6–12in) apart, depending on the size of the plant.

Thin to 10cm (4in) spacings within the rows when the seedlings are about 2.5cm (1in) tall. After about a month, transplant the middle two of every four plants into a separate row, to leave the seedlings at 30cm (12in) spacings; this gives them enough room to grow on without competition.

In early September, transplant the young plants to their final flowering site.

Sowing under cover

I've found the Iceland poppies and sweet Williams do better sown under cover with a bit more care (see also Half-hardy annuals, page 88).

(Above) *Euphorbia cyparissias* provides a good base for spring flowers (see p144).

(Overleaf) My favorites! Iceland poppies 'Meadow Pastels' and 'Red Sail'.

Sow two seeds in each cell of a modular tray, or in an expanded peat pellet. Keep them warm, moist and dark until they germinate. As seedlings they like warm roots, cool tops and all-round light.

Pot on the seedlings into 6–9cm (3–3½in) pots when they are large enough to handle.

When the roots have filled the pot, this usually happens by late August or early September, put them out into their final flowering position.

The best biennials to grow

Lots of biennials are cut-and-come-again, and they give you a scale and stature in the garden and the vase which is more difficult to find with the annual group.

Anchusa azurea, Blue alkanet

90cm (3ft)
Climate zones 3–8

Description
A large, robust plant, with the best, brilliant royal blue flowers you'll find. It is, in fact, a short-lived perennial, not strictly speaking a biennial, but is best treated in this way. It gets a bit scrawny if left in place for a third season.

Role
I pick it as filler foliage for a large arrangement (see page 75), or use side-branches as a 'gatecrasher' in a smaller vase.

Good combinations
You won't get a better contrast to white, acid-green, or orange, than this rich, saturated blue, so grow as much of this plant as you can.

Special growing requirements
Needs individual staking. Grow from seed or propagate from root cuttings. When you dig the spent plants up towards the end of summer, cut several 4cm (1½in) sections of root and poke them into pots of moist compost. They'll sprout leaves in less than a month, ready for putting out in the garden in early September. Needs searing.

Anthriscus sylvestris 'Ravenswing', Queen Anne's lace
60cm (2ft)
Climate zones 5–8

Description
A crimson-leaved cow parsley, remarkable for its delicate but bold-colored foliage, rather than its flowers. It is also know as black-leaved cow parsley.

Role
I use the leaves as an upper story in small, bedside table arrangements. It has the perfect architectural shape to add an interesting silhouette to any small glass of flowers (see page 77).

Good combinations
I love this in the spring, with its fine, downy foliage in rich crimson; it stands out brilliantly against the acid-green of euphorbias.

Special growing requirements
Germination can be difficult. The seed must be absolutely fresh. You can sow this straight into the ground, or under cover. They will self-sow. Needs searing.

Campanula medium, Canterbury bells

90cm (3ft)
Climate zones 4–10

Description
The bumper bellflower. This has huge, thimble-shaped flowers, 5cm (2in) long, in deep, rich blue, white, or beautiful pale pink.

Role
This is a bride if there ever was one. It's also wonderful on its own in a large glass vase, one color, or all three together. My husband thinks this is a vulgar plant, hideous and over-blown; I love it.

Good combinations
Float all the colors together in a huge, shallow bowl.

Special growing requirements
It needs netting or staking in April, and then looks superb in the garden or cutting patch until August. You must pick, or dead-head, every 3–4 days to get the longest flowering season. This campanula also makes a wonderful houseplant for two months or more. Sow it straight into the ground, or under cover, and put half in the garden and half in pots for overwintering under cover. These will be in flower by early May. They don't self-sow.

Cynoglossum amabile, Chinese forget-me-not
45cm (18in)
Climate zones 7–11

Description
Wonderful Bahamian-sea-blue flowers above silvery green foliage. This is my solution to the forget-me-not problem, banned from my garden because it self-sows too prolifically. This has larger, richer blue flowers and is in bloom for three times as long. I also grow a pretty pale pink called 'Mystery Rose'.

Role
The perfect bridesmaid with other blues, and a wonderful gate-crasher too.

Good combinations
Mix it with whites and greens, or orange. This is also beautiful with silver and most pinks, soft or strong.

Special growing requirements
If you cut this back at the end of the year, it may give a second flowering season. It can be grown as an annual from an early sowing, but forms bigger, stronger plants when treated as a biennial. Needs searing.

Dianthus barbatus 'Albus', Sweet William

45cm (18in)
Climate zones 3–7

Description
Pure white flowers mixed with spiky, apple-green buds and stems, the color of 'Golden Delicious' apples.

Role
The flowers make brilliant fillers in any arrangement. Use the spiky buds as an upper story in spring arrangements; they're especially good for an acid-green and white theme.

Good combinations
Lovely arranged with sweet peas, *Lathyrus odoratus*, and lime-green *Alchemilla mollis*.

Special growing requirements
Cut back after flowering, and it will flower for another season, and the plants are just as vigorous and productive.

Dianthus barbatus
'Homeland'
Sweet William
45cm (18in)
Climate zones 3–7

Description
This has nearly the richness of color and velvety petals of the Nigrescens Group (see right), but with a white eye in the center of the flower. It looks like an auricula, those lovely spring flowering primulas that I would grow lots of, if they took less time. *D. barbatus* 'Crimson Auricula-eyed' is similar.

Role
The flowers make brilliant fillers in any rich-colored arrangement, but make the strongest statement used alone against an acid-green foliage base. Use the spiky buds as well. I use these as an upper story in spring arrangements.

Good combinations
Beautiful arranged as the only flower in an alchemilla or euphorbia base, with a few stems of cerinthe added too.

Special growing requirements
If you cut this back after flowering, it will flower for another season.

Dianthus barbatus
Nigrescens Group
(syn. 'Nigricans'),
Sweet William
45cm (18in)
Climate zones 3–7

Description
The best sweet William I know. It has velvet flowers of almost black crimson and a faint clove scent. I love it in a generous block in the garden where the evergreen foliage – dark-green washed with crimson – looks good all year.

Role
The flowers make brilliant fillers – the perfect bridesmaids – in any rich-colored arrangement. Pick the spiky, sea-urchin-like buds as well. I use these as an upper story in spring flower arrangements.

Good combinations
For a rich Venetian combination, arrange this with orange, or go for black and white, combining it with sweet peas – the almost black *Lathryus odoratus* 'Black Knight', and cream *L. odoratus* 'Mrs Collier' – as well as the most highly scented plant I grow, the stock or gillyflower, *Matthiola*, in its white perennial form (see page 26).

Special growing requirements
If you cut this back after flowering, it will flower for another season, or even two, and the plants are just as strong.

Dianthus barbatus
'Oeschberg',
Sweet William
45cm (18in)
Climate zones 3–7

Description
I love this brilliant magenta sweet William with a crimson flush to the leaves and stems. It's bright and rich – you can't miss it.

Role
The flowers and foliage make good fillers in any rich-colored arrangement. Pick the spiky, sea-urchin-like buds as well, and use them as an upper story in spring flower arrangements.

Good combinations
Mix this with other deep pinks and orange. I pick it with euphorbia, the raspberry-red cornflower, *Centaurea cyanus* 'Red Boy' and the deep orange marigold, *Calendula officinalis* 'Indian Prince'.

Special growing requirements
Cut back after flowering, and it will flower for another season, and the plants are just as vigorous and productive.

Digitalis purpurea
f. *albiflora*,
White foxglove
1.2m (4ft)
Climate zones 4–8

Description
There are lots of biennial foxgloves, but my favorite is this pure, creamy white. I have it planted as bedding all around the farmyard at home. Planted in early autumn, it quickly creates a lush edge of bright green that looks good all the way through the winter, whatever the weather.

Role
Use them as the vertical spike in an arrangement, or arrange them in a large glass vase on their own.

Good combinations
Mix them with bosomy peonies, or with the statuesque Giant thistle (*Onopordon acanthium*), sweet rocket (*Hesperis matronalis*) and the pale Iceland poppies (*Papaver nudicaule* 'Meadow Pastels').

Special growing requirements
Foxgloves thrive in sun or shade. Seed can be sown direct into the ground, or under cover. They have tiny seeds and are fiddly to sow. They will self-sow. A few may revert to the ordinary pink shade, but you can tweak out any seedlings with pink-tinged midribs.

Eryngium giganteum,
'Miss Willmott's
Ghost', Sea holly
60cm (2ft)
Climate zones 6–8

Description
This is one of the best forms of sea holly and it is very easy to grow. The flowerhead looks like an egg surrounded by a spiky ruff of bright silver. A superb architectural plant, freely self-seeding from one year to another.

Role
One of my favorite foliage bases for midsummer. Sadly, it is one of the few biennials that is not cut-and-come-again, so make sure you've got lots of it. Then you can pick some for inside and leave some in the garden too.

Good combinations
The silvery color and strong structure combine well with anything.

Special growing requirements
The seeds must be fresh: weeks, not months old. There is no point sowing seed that has been stored from the year before, so make sure you're buying this year's seed. I harvest ours in July and August. Sow direct, or under cover, but plant them out when still small. The tap root dislikes disturbance.

Erysimum cheiri,
Wallflower

45cm (18in)
Climate zones 5–9

Description
These plants have a maiden aunt image that is undeserved. Grow the tall cultivars in single colors, then you'll get glamorous, velvety flowers in crimson, with *E. cheiri* 'Blood Red'; flame-red, *E. c.* 'Fireking'; and magenta, *E. c.* 'Violet'. They have a beautiful scent, and are superb in the spring garden, for filling gaps between tulips and euphorbias.

Role
The best bridesmaids you can grow. Pick them with hyacinths and tulips in all colors, shapes and sizes.

Good combinations
Use 'Blood Red' with burgundy tulips or hyacinths, 'Fireking' with *Tulipa* 'Ballerina' and 'Violet' with the brilliant pink *Anemone coronaria* 'Orchid' (see page 135).

Special growing requirements
You can sow them direct into the ground, or under cover. They don't self-sow. The small, shiny, black flea beetle can be a pest with these, leaving holes in the flowers and leaves. If it is a major problem, cover the plants with horticultural fleece to form a physical barrier.

Euphorbia lathyris,
Caper spurge

90cm (3ft)
Climate zones 7–9

Description
This euphorbia looks very different to the others, without the acid-green that is so characteristic of the genus. It stands about a meter (3ft) high, with amazing, angular flowers – like the eyes of a chameleon. After picking, the new growth at the stem tip turns from a rather dull, grey-green to that brilliant acid-green, but you must keep picking regularly to get this.

Role
It's a superb filler, or upper-story foliage plant; one of the best architectural foliage plants I grow.

Good combinations
Mix it with any color, blues and whites, or in combination with strong oranges, purples and blues.

Special growing requirements
It self-sows, some say too prolifically, but is easy to transplant to where you want it, as long as you move it when small.

**(Opposite)
Sweet rocket and anchusa with a splash of orange Iceland poppy, behind.**

Hesperis matronalis,
Dame's violet,
Sweet rocket
90cm (3ft)
Climate zones 3–8

Description
The lovely sweet rocket is no relation to the rocket you eat in salad. It's a tall plant, covered in simple mauve flowers, or white ones in *H. matronalis* var. *albiflora*; both have a sweet honey scent.

Role
Pick it for arranging on its own in a large glass vase for a fireplace, or use it as a foliage base for other, showier flowers. The seedpods make an excellent filler, looking like fine French beans at the end of every flower stem (see page 75).

Good combinations
I love the mauve with white foxgloves (*Digitalis purpurea* f. *albiflora*) and pale Iceland poppies (*Papaver nudicaule*). It also looks good with brighter colors, such as orange, or the blue of Anchusa. The clouds of white flowers look lovely with spires of white foxgloves.

Special growing requirements
Sweet rocket thrives in sun or shade. Plant it in great drifts in dark corners beneath trees or shrubs. You can do this if you're growing plants from seed, as you'll have plenty of seedlings.

Lunaria annua,
Honesty

90cm (3ft)
Climate zones 4–8

Description
Lunaria annua 'Munstead Purple' are rich red-purple flowers, those of *L. annua* var. *albiflora* are pure white. They are both mainstays of the spring cutting garden, providing tall and bulky stems for large arrangements from the end of March.

Role
Don't just pick the flowers in spring, use the green seed cases too, in early summer. They make one of the best upper storys and foliage fillers you can grow. The fresh pods of the white-flowered form are pure, bright green; the purple-flowered ones have a purple wash over the green, so pick them fresh; they become silvery when dry.

Good combinations
In flower, these both make wonderful flowery bases for hyacinths and tulips (see page 76). I also pick the purple and mix it with the shrubby *Euphorbia characias* in a huge glass vase.

Special growing requirements
Very easy and will grow almost anywhere – sun or shade, damp or dry. Best grown from fresh seed. It will self-sow.

Onopordum acanthium, Giant thistle, Scotch thistle
2.5–3m (7–10ft)
Climate zones 7–9

Description
I'd been growing this in my garden as a windbreak for years before I picked it. It does indeed make the perfect windbreak. If stoutly staked, a line of them will take a battering and filter the wind to give shelter over 6–10m (20–30ft).

Role
It's also a dramatic, architectural foliage plant for flower arranging. Use it as a foliage base, or cut a few flowering stems and add them as an upper story.

Good combinations
The silvery leaves and silver and purple, thistle-like flowerheads go with any color.

Special growing requirements
You need thorn-proof gloves to pick them. The texture of the leaves is smooth and velvety, but there are lethal spikes around the leaf edges. Sear the stems ends. If you cut stems over 75cm (30in) high, sear a good 5cm (2in) at the bottom of the stem. They will self-sow.

Papaver nudicaule 'Meadow Pastels', Iceland poppy
60cm (2ft)
Climate zones 7–9

Description
The perfect flowers, which look delicate and frail, last a week in water and bloom for three to four months in the garden. This cultivar is scented as well, strongest in the paler colors. My favourite plant, this cultivar has huge, saucer-sized flowers.

Role
Arrange it on its own, twenty stems cut to different heights in a simple pewter jug (see page 72), or use it as a bride in any arrangement.

Good combinations
I love the pale colors with whites, pinks and blues, and the golds and oranges with a more Venetian mix of purple, blue and acid-green.

Special growing requirements
Superb biennial plants, but one of the most temperamental to grow from seed. They should be sown under cover, not straight into the ground, and even with this extra attention you'll lose some to damping off. For thirty plants that germinate, you'll probably only plant out half of them. Needs searing.

Papaver nudicaule 'Red Sail', Iceland poppy
60cm (2ft)
Climate zones 7–9

Description
This is the equal of 'Meadow Pastels', but in a single color, rich red-orange, so it's easier to integrate into a general planting scheme. The flowers are not scented.

Role
Arrange it on its own, twenty stems cut to different heights in a simple pewter jug or use it as a bride in any arrangement (see page 139).

Good combinations
This looks superb with magenta, with the blue of cornflowers (*Centaurea cyanus*), and with dark, rich crimson of the almost black sweet William (*Dianthus barbatus* Nigrescens Group).

Special growing requirements
Superb biennial plants, but one of the most temperamental to grow from seed. They should be sown under cover, not straight into the ground, and even with this extra attention you'll lose some to damping off. For thirty plants that germinate, you'll probably only plant out half of them. Needs searing.

half-hardy annuals

An annual is a plant that lives for one year, forming roots and leaves, flowering and setting seed all within twelve months. If it's half-hardy, it cannot withstand winter wet and cold, and will be killed by the frosts.

The indispensables

You can't do without half-hardy annuals in your cutting patch. If hardy annuals are the backbone to the cutting garden, these are the frills – they're some of the most glamorous cut flowers you can grow. It's in their texture that many of them excel. Hold the snapdragon, *Antirrhinum* 'Night and Day', up to the light. The buds, stem tips and base of the flowers have a waxy sheen, with the surface covered in tiny, iridescent hairs, as if each one has been dusted with glitter. And with all the dark and strong colored snapdragons, both the top and bottom lip of the flower has the finest velvet texture.

Snapdragons aren't the only ones with this opulent feel. Look at the orange Mexican sunflower (*Tithonia rotundifolia* 'Torch'), the Moroccan blue sage *Salvia patens*, and the lime-green and deep red cultivars of the tobacco plant (*Nicotiana*) (see page 84). You won't find such richly textured petals anywhere else.

The long, the short and the tall

Many half-hardy annuals are statuesque and impressive in scale. They shoot up to 2m (6ft) or more, in a matter of weeks. One of my favorites is the huge, pink-trumpeted *Nicotiana tabacum*. Its leaves are like elephant's ears in brilliant apple green. I love it mixed with dahlias; their dressy flowers are a good match to the size and showiness of the tobacco. It goes on to have apple green seed pods from late summer onwards, invaluable for their fresh brightness towards the end of the picking season. Other tobacco plants are prone to mosaic virus, which can wipe out your whole crop in a couple of weeks, but this one seems resistant.

Love-lies-bleeding (*Amaranthus caudatus*) gives you texture and scale on the same stem. I love the green-flowered cultivar, *A. caudatus* 'Viridis', with its cascades of green tassels in soft chenille. Best of all though are the crimson-leaved and flowered *Amaranthus* 'Intense Purple' and 'Hopi Red Dye'. They look similar, but the latter is the darkest (rich black-crimson) and it grows to about half the height of the giant 'Intense Purple'. Pick the side branches, or the main stem for a great arrangement of crimson, acid-green and orange. They are some of the best filler foliage plants you can have.

So you've got tall, but you also want short. I like growing a few plants for small arrangements for putting beside my bed or in the bathroom, and for this you want zinnias. Pick the single color *Zinnia* 'Cactus Orange' and mix it with blue, or the easy to grow and prolific *Zinnia* Sprite Series. Combine all the colors – magenta, pink, gold and orange – with a few rich-colored *Salpiglossis* and snapdragons thrown in and you'll have a sumptuous, Titianesque-toned arrangement in minutes. It will look good for over a week (see page 90).

The right stuff

Half-hardy annuals make wonderful cut flowers. Like the hardies, they are cut-and-come-again and they bloom for longer than any other group of flowering plants. Only dahlias can compete with their four or five month productive season. Think of the classic bedding plants sold in strips at garden centers all around the country in the spring. They're popular because they flower for so long, filling tubs and hanging baskets with color throughout the summer and autumn. You can buy petunias, pansies, trailing lobelia, snapdragons and nicotianas as mini-plants, but there's a much richer selection if you grow them from seed.

What you'll find in bedding strips are mixed colors and dwarf forms, specially bred for containers. These are not what you want as cut flowers. Single colors with tall stems are the ideal and that's what you'll get if you choose cut flower forms. With a good stock of half-hardy annuals, you'll have buckets and buckets of brilliant color to bring into the house from July until October, with some flowering well on into the late autumn and the first hard frost. In the cutting garden here last year, the first frost was late and we had a bed of *Cleome*, the American spider flower, still spectacular and zinging with color until early November.

The glamorous, glitzy
Antirrhinum 'Night and Day'.

How to grow half-hardy annuals

The two most important things to remember are to grow the seedlings in a light, frost-free place, and to protect them under cover until the frosts are over. You'll then have decent-sized plants, nearly in flower, ready to put out in the garden at the end of spring. These are my six keys to success to sowing under cover.

1 Don't sow too early

I used to start sowing my half-hardy annual seed in late winter (February). I was chomping at the bit, longing to be getting some plants on the go. For several reasons, I now wait until early spring (March) for a few early plants and the beginning of April for everything else. An early April sowing gives six weeks between sowing and the last frosts. (Make it mid-April if you live in colder areas than mine.) This is the perfect length of time for quick-growing annuals to form decent-sized plants ready to go out into the garden. Depending on the plant, they should be in flower one to two months later.

February sowing is now out of bounds and here are the reasons why. Seeds sown later make healthier, bushier plants. As spring progresses, light levels and temperatures increase; temperatures also fluctuate less between night and day. All of these factors allow cold-sensitive plants to grow vigorously, and healthy, well-grown plants grow and flower much more quickly once they're out in the garden. February-sown seeds make leggy, collapsing things.

Plants sown later in the spring soon catch up with an early sowing. With most half-hardy annuals, seedlings sown in early March will be the same size as those sown a month later by the time you plant them out.

I raise all my half-hardy seedlings in a polytunnel with heated propagator blankets as the only source of heat. I do live in the south of England and garden at 140m (450ft) altitude, so my climate is milder than most in North America. If you don't have limitless room, the ideal scenario is to have the roots of your seedlings just filling a 7–9cm (3–3½in) pot by the time the frosts are over in your region. Any bigger and you will have a problem storing them until the frosts are finished. Any smaller and the seedlings won't thrive when put outside to fend for themselves. In informal trials here, I've found that this size of pot is the ideal, partly because the plants are small enough to transplant without being checked by their move. So allow six weeks between sowing and the expected last frost date; your local gardening center or club will help you out on this. If you sow in modular trays, most can be planted into 9cm (3½in) pots about a month later and left to get on with it until they go out into the garden. If you sow earlier, you'll have to do another stage of potting on and will create unnecessary work and pressure on space.

There are a few exceptions. Antirrhinums, *Cobaea scandens*, *Leonotis leonurus*, *Verbena bonariensis* and *Salvia patens* are all really perennials. They're grown as half-hardy annuals because they are very productive in their first year. With the exception of *Verbena bonariensis*, they are so tender, I'd have to overwinter them inside. As perennials, they are on a slower time scale than annual plants and will take longer to germinate and grow to flowering size. I sow them in early March, about a month earlier than the rest.

Certain plants, particularly cleomes and *Moluccella laevis*, need quite high temperatures to germinate quickly. I set the propagator at 25°C (77°F) for these and I sow them later than everything else so the ambient temperature is higher too. Zinnias are also sown last. They hate root disturbance and are best planted out when still small.

(Opposite) I love the orange-black contrast of *Cosmos sulphureus* 'Bright Lights' with *Scabiosa atropurpurea*.

(Below) *Zinnia* 'Cactus Orange' with *Salvia patens*, *Nicotiana alata* 'Lime Green' and *Ageratum* 'Florist's Blue'.

2 Sow thinly

The less competition your seedlings have from close neighbors, the better. If you cram small plants together, they'll be forced to compete for light, water and nutrients and will not do well. Closely packed, they may think they're on the way out and will try and reproduce as quickly as they can. They bolt – run up to flower and seed, without filling out.

Sow seed as thinly as you can. You can sow into traditional seed trays, trying to place seed individually when you can, but I now sow almost everything in modular trays. This year, I've experimented with sowing into expanded peat pellets. They work well, saving a lot of time, but I worry about the environmental costs and am trying to find a peat-free alternative. If you pot them on as soon as the roots have filled the module, it avoids competition between neighboring plants and you skip the time-consuming and fiddly stage of pricking out the seedlings.

To germinate most half-hardy seeds, you want a warm, moist, dark environment. I place my seed trays on a propagator bench at 20°C (68°F). I cover them with empty compost bags to enclose moisture and warmth and exclude light. I check morning and evening for any sign of germination. Trays must be uncovered and put in a place of maximum light from then on. Cleomes are the exception amongst the plants I grow. They need bright light to germinate and will do nothing in the dark. These seeds need to be surface sown. If you don't have a propagator, you can germinate all but cleome seeds in an airing cupboard, and grow on your seedlings on a cool, but very light windowsill. Water them sparingly – the compost should never be saturated.

Once germinated, good light levels, cool air temperatures and warm roots are needed. All-round light is important in forming strong, bulky plants. Seedlings grown on here in a lean-to greenhouse are twice as leggy as those stored in the polytunnel.

3 Pot on in good time

Never let your plants become pot-bound. Pot on as soon as you see white roots appearing at the holes in the bottom of the pot. A pot-bound plant never quite recovers. Inevitably, I seem to have a few pot-bound plants hanging around at the end of the planting-out season. Don't put them in the ground as they are. Pot-bound, they sulk and continue to think they've run out of space and food and, if they do resume growth, it will probably be to bolt skywards and produce seed. Be brutal – rip the bottom of the root ball off the plant. This shocks them into good growth again straight away.

4 Pinch out and plant out pronto

Pinch out and plant out into the garden as soon as the frosts are over. With any plants that are beginning to look leggy, rather than bushy – one central, spindly, vertical stem shooting up to the skies – pinch out the tip. This means breaking off the central stem between your thumb and forefinger, leaving at least two buds on the stem below your cut, to bulk out and create a shorter, stronger plant. Do this before planting out.

5 Teamwork and delegation

It's best to get everything out into the garden in one go, so you don't have plants hanging around getting pot-bound or sitting baking inside. If you can, rope in the whole family or get some friends together to help you. The sooner your seedlings are planted in the garden, the sooner you'll have a crop of flowers.

6 Stake your plants

It is important to stake and support your plants. You can use netting for fine-stemmed plants and canes for tall, stout-stemmed ones with heavy heads (see page 132).

(Opposite) One of my favourite multi-stemmed vases with wonderful, velvet textured flowers (see p144).

(Inset) *Rudbeckia Rustic*. This is one of the most robust and easy half-hardies.

(Overleaf) The cutting garden in summer, full of sweet peas, half-hardy annuals, and *Stipa gigantea* (a perennial grass).

Sowing the seed

Fill trays or modules with fine, non-lumpy, multi-purpose potting compost and firm gently to get rid of any large air pockets. The surface level should reach about 1cm (½in) below the top to allow room for watering. Water the compost before sowing as thinly as you can, placing individual seeds where possible. If you're sowing into modules or expanded peat pellets, sow two seeds to a cell. If both germinate, uproot one. If the seed is too small for this, put some in the palm of your hand and sow as few in each as you can. Tweezers are a good idea for tiny seeds. Don't pour straight from the packet or your palm. This creates clumps of crowded seedlings and, especially under glass, they are much more likely to succumb to a fungal disease, damping off or botrytis.

Cover the seed with a very thin layer of compost. Leave tiny seeds uncovered. No need to water again, just cover the tray with a plastic compost bag. Label them with name and date of sowing.

Aftercare

Check twice a day for signs of green. Remove the cover as soon as the first shoots appear and place in a cool, bright place. If you are unlikely to check for germination every day, leave the trays uncovered.

If you've sown into conventional seed trays, you'll need to separate seedlings into individual pots (prick out) when they have two pairs of leaves. Hold the leaves, never the stems or roots. Tease the roots apart and plant each in its own pot. Plant deeply, covering the roots and stem to the level of the seed leaves (the simple pair of leaves that form first). Water them in. pot on into the next size as soon as you see white roots appearing at the holes in the bottom of the pot.

About a week or so before the last frosts are expected, harden them off by gradually exposing them to outside conditions. If you have a cold frame, put them in that and leave the lid off for longer periods each day, otherwise open the greenhouse doors on a similar principle. As soon as the frosts have finished, plant them out in the garden at the distance recommended on the back of the packet. Water in well, with a drench, not a sprinkle, for two weeks so they establish a deep root system that will access the ground water.

The toughest half-hardies

Most half-hardy annuals are best raised under cover, but a few do well if sown directly into the soil outside, as you would hardy annuals. Just sow later when the frosts are over. You can expect most to be in bloom by late summer, but with antirrhinums, leonotis and verbena, it may be early autumn before you see a flower. If you don't have a propagator or greenhouse, these are the ones for you.

Amaranthus caudatus
antirrhinums
Cosmos
Leonotis leonurus
Moluccella laevis
Nicotiana sylvestris
Phlox drummondii
rudbeckias
verbenas
zinnias

Foliage and upper-story half-hardy annuals

Half-hardy annuals are the most productive of cut flowers. You'll need equal quantities of foliage and flowers. Bear this in mind when you select what to grow – choose at least 50 percent basic, filler and upper story foliage plants to make the best arrangements.

(Opposite)
I love this simple fresh color combination – orange, lemon and lime.

Amaranthus caudatus, Love-lies-bleeding

60–90cm (2–3ft)
Climate zones 8–11

Description
Arching, branched stems with shield-shaped leaves in bright green. *A. caudatus* has crimson flowers; *A. caudatus* 'Viridis' has apple-green ones. The tassels gradually elongate as the plants develop. I grow lots of the green.

Role
Excellent foliage plant; it is late maturing, coming into its own in late summer and autumn. Use it as the foliage base for a large arrangement, or pick side branches for a smaller vase. I love the tassels hanging right down on to the table and sprawling out at the base of the vase (see page 124).

Good combinations
Perfect for mixing with dahlias and sunflowers in autumn arrangements. I also use it on its own, ten or fifteen stems arranged in a large glass vase.

Special growing requirements
Easy to grow. They're happy sown under cover or straight into the ground outside once the frosts are over. Needs staking or netting support.

Amaranthus 'Intense Purple'

1.5m (5ft)
Climate zones 8–11

Description
Shield-shaped leaves with more upright tassels than *A. caudatus* in rich crimson. 'Hopi Red Dye' is the darkest crimson-black, with ruby red stems. It makes shorter plants, to 90cm (3ft). Both are superb. I have 'Hopi Red Dye' in four large pots at the center of the garden this year.

Role
There is no better primary or filler foliage for bold arrangements than either of these two plants. If you keep picking, they will continue to bush out.

Good combinations
Wonderful as the foliage in a black and white arrangement and perfect for mixing with other crimson-blacks, orange and acid-green (see page 137).

Special growing requirements
Easy to grow. If you have no room to raise plants under cover, you can still grow these. They're happy sown straight into the ground outside once the frosts are over. *A.* 'Intense Purple' self-sows in my garden. Needs support.

Moluccella laevis, Bells of Ireland

60cm (2ft)
Climate zones 4–9

Description
Vertical spires with seven or eight bright apple-green cups, arranged in whorls at intervals up the stem.

Role
This is a strong contender for being my favorite foliage plant. I love the twists and turns of the stem, which add movement, in a brilliant color, to any bunch of flowers.

Good combinations
Use this with all colors – calm and pale, or rich and bright.

Special growing requirements
Germination may be slow. This is improved by placing the seed packet in the deep freeze for a week before you sow. Set the propagator at 20°C (68°F) and keep covered until germination occurs. They do well from sowing under cover in April, or direct sowing in early May. It's a very long-lasting cut flower, with a vase life of over two weeks. Remove all, or most, of the leaves. They obscure the flowers and age much more quickly than the rest. It will dry, hung upside-down tied with a rubber band. Will self-sow. Needs staking.

Nicotiana tabacum, Tobacco plant

1.8–2.2m (6–7ft)
Climate zones 7–9

Description
A statuesque tobacco plant whose leaves can grow to over half a meter (20in) in the brightest, freshest, apple-green. Flowers at the end of summer with pink trumpets at the end of swollen, bright green calyces, like green cheesy footballs gathered together on a stem. This is actual tobacco – the plant grown as a crop all over the Mediterranean and U.S.A. to be smoked in cigarettes.

Role
One of the best garden and cut flower foliage plants for late summer and autumn.

Good combinations
Arrange five stems, with leaves, on their own in a plain glass vase. The leaves and seedpods are wonderful used as foliage with dahlias, cosmos and cleomes in autumn.

Special growing requirements
Easy to grow in full sun. I plant it in large groups amongst dahlias where it looks good into the autumn. It seems to have resistance to tobacco mosaic virus so is a good one to choose. Needs staking.

Perilla frutescens

60cm (2ft)
Climate zones 7–9

Description
Sumptuous black-crimson leaves, which are highly cut and ruffled, like handfuls of creased silk-satin on a stem. It has green, crimson-washed stems in contrast to the leaves. If you keep picking the leaves, you won't get the insignificant flowers.

Role
Use this as filler foliage with bright acid-green, or silver cardoon leaves.

Good combinations
It makes a wonderful combination with the similar-colored *Salpiglossis* 'Chocolate' – same color, same texture and similar shape.

Special growing requirements
Easy to grow. Sear the stem ends in boiling water. Needs staking.

My favorite half-hardy flowers

People are put off by half-hardy annuals which need raising under cover. Don't be. You'll have fifty vases of cosmos or rudbeckia in one season and they couldn't be easier to grow.

Antirrhinum,
Snapdragon

60cm (2ft)
Climate zones 1–11

Description
Excellent, well-known cutting annual. Very long flowering and a long vase life. Grow it in crimson, scarlet, coral-pink, and white. The F1 Liberty Hybrids are good in these colors. They have tall stems. My favorites are 'Scarlet Giant' which fades to a lovely deep tomato-soup orange, and 'Night and Day', a white-throated, deep crimson that looks as if every flower is cut from silk velvet.

Role
These make some of the best summer brides.

Good combinations
Use *A.* 'Night and Day' and a white cultivar in a black and white vase. Mix the crimson and 'Scarlet Giant' with crimson dahlias, *Tithonia rotundifolia* and euphorbia (see page 124).

Special growing requirements
They take longer to germinate and are slower to grow, so sow your snapdragons first of all half-hardies in early March. Some have a tendency to rust, but those described have better resistance than most. Needs support.

Cleome hassleriana,
American spider flower

90cm (3ft)
Climate zones 4–11

Description
Lovely tall, airy, late-flowering, unusual and elegant plant. Grown for cutting by the Victorians. White: 'Helen Campbell' Purple: 'Violet Queen' Deep pink: 'Cherry Queen' Paler pink: 'Pink Queen' They're still looking good in late autumn.

Role
Ethereal brides for large arrangements and very good, one stem on its own in a tall narrow vase. Will look good for ten days.

Good combinations
Arrange the pink with *Nicotiana tabacum, Euphorbia schillingii* and pinky-orange dahlias, such as 'Raffles'. Arrange the white on its own, or in a large vase with *Cosmos bipinnatus* 'Purity'. The purple is good with orange *Tithonia rotundifolia.*

Special growing requirements
Can be tricky and slow to germinate. You need fresh seed, sown in good light and lots of warmth (at least 20°C/68°F). Pot on, pinch out and plant out promptly It has thorns on the stems. Remove these as you condition them. Needs support.

Cobaea scandens,
Cup and saucer plant
Can grow to 20m (70ft) in the wild.
Climate zones 9–11

Description
Large, cup-shaped flowers with a prominent green calyx around the base. This gives this plant its common name. They are creamy green at first then purple later; there is a creamy white form, *C. scandens* f. *alba.*

Role
Arrange a few stems on their own, for a bedside table vase. It's also one of the best plants for floating in a large shallow bowl. Scatter nightlights in between.

Good combinations
Mix the white with *Cosmos bipinnatus* 'Purity' for a small, simple vase. I love the purple with orange, *Tithonia rotundifolia* 'Torch'.

Special growing requirements
This is a tender climbing perennial not an annual, perfect for covering a greenhouse wall. I grow it outside over arches and frames in the garden. It can withstand one or two degrees of frost, so I try to get it out at the beginning of May to give you flowers by August. It goes on flowering until late autumn in Sussex.

Cosmos bipinnatus

1.2–1.5m (4–5ft)
All zones

Description
Simple, straightforward, pretty flowers with five or six petals arranged around a golden heart. *C. bipinnatus* 'Dazzler' is rich carmine; 'Purity' is white and it has fresh-green, feathery leaves. I also love the good mix of oranges and yellows in *C. sulphureus* 'Bright Lights'.

Role
Very versatile flowers.

Good combinations
Use 'Purity' in a glass vase on its own. Its lovely foliage complements the flowers. Without the flowers, the foliage is useful too. I pick *C. sulphureus* 'Bright Lights' for bunches in the colors of oranges, lemons and limes (see page 94).

Special growing requirements
Cosmos 'Purity' is the easiest plant to germinate and grow. Sow in April. *C. sulphureus* can be trickier, but happily self-seeds in my garden. They don't last as well when cut as the *C. bipinnatus* cultivars. Sear the stem ends, but even then, these flowers will only last 3 or 4 days. Needs staking.

Leonotis leonurus,
Lion's ear

2.5m (8ft)
Climate zones 9–11

Description
An unusual, towering plant, which puts up thin, straight stems with tiers of orange, salvia-like flowers in whorls from top to bottom.

Role
The perfect vertical, upper story for large arrangements.

Good combinations
Mix it with rich crimsons and oranges – dahlias, tithonias and amaranthus in the garden and in the vase.

Special growing requirements
A tender perennial plant that can be grown as an annual. Sow it earlier than the rest. It is slower to grow. Sear stem ends. If you sear at least a tenth the height of the stem, it will be upstanding, right to the tip, whatever the length of stem. Self-sows in a sheltered spot in my garden. Needs support.

Nicotiana, Tobacco plants

Varying heights
Climate zones 7–9

Description

Lovely velvet flowers. Grow *N.* x *sanderae*, particularly for green and deep red. The deep red has a lovely night scent. Purple varieties fade to a dull mauve – not so good. Whites and pale pinks tend to flop and close in the heat of the day and look too scraggy for flower arranging. Also grow acid-green *N. langsdorffii* or *N. rustica*. They are taller plants with smaller flowers. I love *N. sylvestris*, a huge, stately, white, scented, late-flowering plant.

Role

The acid-green, *N.* 'Lime Green' is one of my all-time favorite filler-flowers (see pages 8 and 94). *N. langsdorffii* and *N. rustica* are airy flowers, both perfect as an upper story to add the final touch to delicate arrangements.

Special growing requirements

Easy to grow. *N.* x *sanderae* cultivars and *N. sylvestris* have a tendency to succumb to a mosaic virus. This starts as a yellow dappling on the back of the leaves. The virus will eventually kill the plant. Remove those affected and burn.

Phlox drummondii, Annual phlox

30–45cm (12–18in)
Climate zones 3–10

Description

Typical phlox flowers on short, stocky plants. *P. drummondii* 'Tapestry Mix' is my favorite mixed color form. It comes in a lovely range of colors – pinks, whites, purples and deep reds with single and bicolored flowers. You can find single color forms, but they tend to be too short to make excellent cut flowers. Sadly, these annual phlox have less scent than the perennial forms, but they're very long flowering and productive.

Role

Excellent for mixed bunches, or for arranging on their own in a small Moroccan tea glass for putting beside your bed.

Good combinations

Pick out the separate colors and mix them with scabious, cosmos, zinnias and other simple, country-style flowers.

Special growing requirements

Very easy. This plant is the most productive of cut flowers in summer and early autumn. The stems have a longer vase life than any I know. Only *Moluccella laevis* can compete.

Rudbeckia Rustic Colour Hybrids

30cm (18in)
Climate zones 3–7

Description

There are lots of rudbeckias in gold and yellow; the daisy-like flowers have narrow petals around a prominent central boss. This variety is my favorite with each flower either wholly or partly colored mahogany brown. They have a wonderful velvet texture too.

Role

This makes a good bridesmaid to other deep-red, crimson-black, and mahogany-colored flowers. It's also lovely brightened up with acid-green.

Good combinations

Pick this with a sunflower such as *Helianthus annuus* 'Deep Red'. It's also lovely with *Helenium* 'Moerheim Beauty'.

Special growing requirements

One of the easiest half-hardy annuals you can grow. It's indestructible.

Tithonia rotundifolia, Mexican sunflower

1.2m (4ft)
Climate zones 5–10

Description

Lovely orange, mini-sunflowers with one of the richest velvet textures of any plant I grow. Flowering from late summer onwards.

Role

I love this plant and it is an excellent bit of glamour for late picking. Use it as a bride or gatecrasher with other velvet-textured flowers.

Good combinations

Combine it with *Salvia patens*, *Nicotiana* 'Lime Green' and dark-colored antirrhinums for a sumptuous, silken, velvet vase (see pages 84 and 90).

Special growing requirements

This is a native Mexican plant that likes it hot. It tends to damp off in the greenhouse if you over water and does not do well in years where light levels are poor. Don't sow it until mid-April, when light levels have increased. Take care of the necks as you arrange them, they bruise and break easily at the base of the flower. Needs staking

---

Verbena bonariensis

1.2m (4ft)
Climate zones 6–9

Description

A haze of purple flowers standing at shoulder height. Lovely in the garden forming an aisle planted down both sides of a path.

Role

Good as the upper story for late-summer and autumn arrangements. Mix it with tall *Nicotiana sylvestris*, *N. tabacum* and the tall grass, *Stipa gigantea*.

Good combinations

It makes wonderful airy vases with any of the grasses – *Panicum miliaceum* 'Violaceum' or *Stipa gigantea*.

Special growing requirements

This perennial is particularly short-lived on a heavy clay soil. It won't overwinter in my garden, so I sow it every year. On a lighter soil, it will survive for a couple of years. Self-sows.

Zinnia elegans

45cm (18in) or more
All zones

Description

Simple, brightly colored flowers. Grow each and every one. Go for single color, cactus-flowered forms in shades of orange; green as in 'Envy', and deep red. And grow the small-flowered, mixed colors of the easy and productive 'Sprite Series'.

Role

Pick 15 or 20 stems and collect them in a tight-headed posy, bound together with ribbon.

Good combinations

Mix them with other rich, Venetian colors – antirrhinums, salpiglossis and salvias (see page 86).

Special growing requirements

Sow in the greenhouse in mid-April, a little later than most half-hardies. Sow into modular trays so you won't need to prick out. They don't like root disturbance, so plant them out when they're still small. Or sow direct into the ground in early May. They suffer from damping off and botrytis in a damp spring, and slugs love the seedlings, so sow more than you need.

97

summer bulbs

✿ Alliums, lilies, eremurus and gladioli are all summer-flowering. You have to grow some summer-flowering bulbs. They may be the most expensive plants in your cutting patch, but they're indispensable. It's like extravagance in your life. Once you've tasted it, once you've felt its rush, there's no doing without it. ✿

The must-have bulbs

Alliums and lilies have a classic swollen, onion-like, underground food store, a true bulb. Eremurus, not true bulbs, have strange fleshy roots, more like an octopus with a central, pointy eye and tentacles spreading out all around. With gladioli, it's a corm, a smaller, drier, squatter thing than the others. It looks more like a pebble off the beach than an onion. They're just grouped together for convenience.

Out in the garden and in a vase, lilies give you a raunchy glamour, which it's lovely to have. Think of all those huge flowers, burnt-orange, crimson and yellow, and great white balloons, with their rich, velvety stamens at the core. Imagine them pouring out the scent in every room in your house – a perfume factory, picked from just outside your front door. Lilies are heaven on a stalk.

You've got to have the allium firework display in the garden as well. *Allium hollandicum* 'Purple Sensation' is my favorite. It's big, but not too big, in rich red-purple and it goes on to form seedpods like green disco balls, hundreds of shiny beads in a globe. It flowers at exactly the right time in late May and through June, helping to tide you over a tricky patch in the garden as the tulips end, and before the annuals have come into their own.

I have a problem growing eremurus, the spectacular foxtail lilies, like gold, orange and yellow feather dusters on a stem. They like a good baking in the summer months and will not survive without excellent drainage. If I gardened on sand, or chalk, they'd be everywhere in drifts all through the garden, but they're expensive and only survive for one year or two years on my heavy clay, so I don't buy them often.

Gladioli can be hideous, but they can be marvellous too. I love the fine, small-flowered, magenta *Gladiolus communis* subsp. *byzantinus*. Like *Allium hollandicum* 'Purple Sensation', it flowers at the right time. I first saw this in huge drifts in olive groves in Crete. It was growing with acid-green euphorbia, purple *Lavandula stoechas*, bright blue *Anchusa*, with the occasional wild tulip in a deep satin-red. All mixed up together with the silver olive leaves, you had a flower arrangement on a grand scale.

There are a few large-flowered hybrid gladioli that I like too. I grow the dark, rich colors – deep purples, crimsons and magentas. It's tempting to go for a green, but I've tried several described as green that turn out to be an ugly, hospital-wall yellow. I tend to avoid the ones with curly, ruched edges to the petals. Gladioli don't need any more froth. The straight-edged kinds are both bolder and more graceful.

With one or two tips up your sleeve on which ones to choose, these bulbs are easy to grow and, if planted properly, your investment won't give you a one-minute-wonder. Lilies are expensive and there are some to avoid that tend to flower for one year only. As a good general rule, avoid the highly bred Oriental hybrids unless you garden on very freely drained soil, or you have space to grow them in pots. Plant the right ones and you'll be glad you've got them, because summer after summer, you'll bring buckets of these large scale and magnificent blooms into your house.

Where to buy bulbs

I recommend buying your bulbs from a mail order catalog, not a garden center. The selection is better and they're likely to be in better condition when you get them. They sometimes hang around in garden centers getting baked and dry, then they're no good to anybody (see also page 33).

When to plant

Early-summer bulbs, such as alliums, *Gladiolus communis* and eremurus, are best planted in the early autumn with your narcissi, hyacinths and fritillaries. It's best to get them into the ground in September, while the soil is still warm. They need an extensive root system to flower well, so will benefit from getting into the ground as soon as you can.

Lilies are different. They can be planted at any time during autumn, winter or early spring. If you have a freely drained soil, it is best to get them in the ground in the autumn, but as long as they are in by early spring

(Below) *Allium giganteum*
interplanted with *Lilium*
'Green Magic', *Euphorbia*

schillingii and cardoons.
(Opposite) A hand-tied bunch
of summer bulbs (see p144).

(end of March) they will be fine. On very heavy soils,
March planting gives far better results. Don't worry if the
bulbs have a sprout. Plant them with the sprout just
above ground and, even if it is bent, it will have righted
itself in three to four weeks.

Hybrid gladioli are tender. Strictly speaking, they
shouldn't go out into the garden until the frosts are over
at the end of spring. In the south of England, I get some
planted out before this. I mulch them in a protective
blanket of mushroom compost, 5cm (2in) deep.
Traditionally, large-flowered gladioli are lifted once
they've flowered. I leave mine in the ground, mulch them
deeply and hope for the best.

How to plant

Most bulbs have a pointed and a blunt end. Plant them
pointy end up. I always plant these large bulbs in
clumps of a minimum of three in the case of lilies and
eremurus, more like seven or nine with alliums and
gladioli. Without these numbers, you get a very dotty
effect. All these summer bulbs, except the hybrid
gladioli, are reliably perennial – reappearing for year
after year – so bear this in mind when you choose
where to plant them. If possible, find them a spot in your
perennial beds around the outside of your cutting patch.
Planted there, they're less likely to be dug up or
disturbed when other things go in. Plant them in a spot

(Opposite) Another wonderful mix of purple (*Penstemon* 'Midnight'), orange (*Lilium* 'Fire King'), acid green (*Euphorbia schillingii*) and silver (*Onopordum acanthium*). (Below) The path leading to my office is lined with *Papaver* *orientale* 'May Queen', *Euphorbia palustris* and *Allium hollandicum* 'Purple Sensation'.

in full sun. Some lilies do well in light shade, but not beneath a large shrub or tree. If you want them there, choose those like *Lilium martagon* and its cultivars, which are tough enough to cope, but have no scent.

Dig a hole for all these bulbs (except eremurus) about 15cm (6in) deep. Don't use a bulb planter – it takes too long. I dig out a trench or shallow hole, taking up as much space as I have room for between other plants. Spread a 5cm (2in) layer of grit all over the bottom. Drainage is the most important thing. They all flower better and live longer if the soil is not cold and clammy. For three or five bulbs planted in a group, dig an over-sized hole, 60–75cm (2–2½ft) wide, piling a mixture of grit and soil in the middle. Place your bulbs on the mound. Leave a gap between each bulb, twice the width of the bulb itself, and then cover over, mixing some more grit into the soil as you replace it. Lilies like a rich soil, so spread two or three spadesful of compost over the area and then roughly fork it in.

Once they're in the ground, do not disturb. They flower much better when they're left to get on with it.

You should also plant eremurus on a mound in a hole, setting the crown on top of a heap of sharp sand, grit and soil, with more grit and sand than soil. Dig out a large circle for three bulbs in one place, about 60cm (2ft) across and 30cm (1ft) deep. Spread the roots evenly down the sides of the mound, so that the eye is just below the surface, then cover the crown with grit too, before filling in with a 50:50 grit and soil mix. They will not flower if buried deeply. They do like excellent drainage – poor drainage is probably the most common reason for failure. They need cold to initiate flowering. On very heavy soil, mark each clump with a cane and dig them up once their foliage has died down and dry them out somewhere cool and dry over the winter. They may well rot away if you leave them in the ground.

Feeding

During the spring, all these bulbs will benefit from feeding. I feed lilies three or four times from when they

start sprouting until they flower, about a month apart, using a low-nitrogen, high-potash fertilizer. I also scatter wood ash – again, rich in potash – over them. If you have no wood ash, you can use a high-potash fertilizer; it's the potash that helps produce good flowers.

Picking

When picking lilies and gladioli, leave at least 30cm (12in) of stem behind. The bottom section has most of the leaves, which are essential for photosynthesis and subsequent food storage in the bulb. This encourages longevity and good flower formation for the following year. Alliums and eremurus both have basal leaves, which don't extend up the flower stem, so you're all right cutting these stems to the ground.

My favorite summer bulbs

You need to choose a few summer bulbs to give you a froth of glamour, to admire and pick in the cutting garden.

Allium giganteum

90cm–1.2m (3–4ft)
Climate zones 4–8

Description
Large, globe-shaped flowers with pompons about twice the size of 'Purple Sensation' in mauve-purple. Any bigger and they would end up looking like candyfloss on a stick. Flowers in June/July.

Role
Best arranged on their own, or in a magnificent arrangement with eremurus.

Good combinations
Put them in a straight-sided plain glass vase. I also arrange seven or nine stems in a tall, orange ceramic jug.

Special growing requirements
Easy to grow. The leaves of this allium are one of the first bits of green to appear in the New Year. They die back by early summer when the flowers appear. Change the water regularly. It gets an oniony smell after three or four days, but the flowers will go on looking good for ten.

Allium hollandicum 'Purple Sensation'

60–90cm (2–3ft)
Climate zones 3–8

Description
This is my favorite allium with its rich, deep purple flowers. I grow it for its May and June pompon flowers and the green, bead-like seed cases, which go on looking good until the end of July.

Role
One of the best brides or gatecrashers amongst early summer flowers. It's a relatively cheap bulb to buy.

Good combinations
You can't do better than *Allium hollandicum* 'Purple Sensation' with deep orange-scarlet Iceland poppy 'Red Sail' (see page 82). Then pick the seedpods as filler foliage (see page 103).

Special growing requirements
I've had this lining a main path in my garden leading up to my office door. It's thriving from a planting five years ago and gets better each year. I cut it to the ground at the end of July when the seedpods have all turned brown. The foliage looks messy and brown about a month to six weeks earlier. I usually cut them back in a late spring-clean. This doesn't appear to weaken the bulb.

Allium sphaerocephalon

60cm (2ft)
Climate zones 7–9

Description
Small-flowered, deep purple allium, like a dark-flowered chive on steroids. It flowers later than others, in August and September. It's lovely in bud and in full flower and you can pick the seedheads until they brown.

Role
One of the best upper storys for moderate-sized, late summer or early autumn bunches.

Good combinations
A rich, dark color for sumptuous, Titianesque-style flowers. It also goes well with bright whites and greens.

Special growing requirements
Cheap, easy to grow bulb, which will self-sow a little. It doesn't become an invasive nightmare as some of the smaller-flowered alliums do.

Eremurus, Foxtail lilies

1.2–1.5m (4–5ft)
Climate zones 6–9

Description
Huge spikes like a fox's brush on end. They look spectacular in the garden. They're available in various colors. *E.* 'Brutus' and *E. himalaicus* are white. *E. stenophyllus* subsp. *stenophyllus* is dark yellow. *E. lactiflorus* 'Oase' and *E.* 'Romance' are pink, and my favorite *E.* x *isabellinus* 'Cleopatra' is orange. You can buy a mix, such as the Shelford Hybrids, for a combination of all these colors.

Role
One of the best high summer brides or gatecrashers.

Good combinations
Use it in a brilliant-colored summer bunch with other summer-flowering bulbs – pink lilies, gladioli and alliums (see page 103). They also look spectacular with *Allium giganteum* and on their own, either all colors mixed up together, or just in monochrome.

Special growing requirements
To flower at all, these bulbs need very good drainage and must not be buried deeply.

Gladiolus 'Black Beauty'

90cm (3ft)
Climate zones 9–11

Description
This large-flowered hybrid is a delicious, dark crimson, with a rich texture to match. 'Black Lash' and 'Arabian Night' are similar.

Role
One of the best verticals for large arrangements. Have it on its own, or in a large arrangement with dahlias, sunflowers and amaranthus.

Good combinations
This looks wonderful in a hanging globe with sunflowers or crimson-black dahlias like 'Rip City'. Use a base of euphorbia mixed with a dark-leafed amaranthus.

Special growing requirements
Each stem looks good in the garden for three or four weeks, so try to plant a handful of fifteen or twenty corms at two-week intervals from mid- to late spring, in order to have fresh flower spikes appearing for six weeks or more. Needs support. If you garden on heavy clay or in cold regions, lift them in autumn as you would dahlias.

(Opposite) *Allium giganteum* and *allium sphaerocephalon* with *Tanacetum* 'Isla Gold'.

Gladiolus communis subsp. *byzantinus*

45cm (18in)
Climate zones 5–10

Description
Fine spikes of brilliant magenta flowers, which bloom much earlier than the large-flowered hybrid kinds. This is my favorite gladiolus, bright, elegant and not too large.

Role
You can use this in almost any role – bride or gatecrasher in a small bunch, or as a bridesmaid with lilies and larger flowers.

Good combinations
A wonderful color with orange, pink and acid-green (see page 103). Excellent as the bride in early summer bunches with a bridesmaid of the magenta cornflower, *Centaurea cyanus* 'Red Boy', or similar-colored sweet William, *Dianthus barbatus* 'Oeschberg'.

Special growing requirements
Easy to grow, perennial bulb. Make sure you get the right one. Lots of companies sell the wild form, with smaller, paler pink flowers. It's not as showy and fine.

Gladiolus 'Fidelio'

90cm (3ft)
Climate zones 7–11

Description
A large-flowered hybrid gladiolus with deep pink, magenta flowers with a straight edge to the petals. The buds and petals have the texture of velvet.

Role
One of the best verticals for large arrangements. Have it on its own, or in a large arrangement with dahlias, sunflowers and amaranthus.

Good combinations
Wonderful with acid-green *Euphorbia schillingii* and *Hydrangea arborescens* 'Annabelle'. Combine them with an orange or deep crimson dahlia.

Special growing requirements
Each stem looks good for three or four weeks, so try to plant a handful of fifteen or twenty corms at two-week intervals from mid- to late spring, in order to have fresh flower spikes appearing for six weeks or more. If you garden on heavy clay or in cold regions, lift them in autumn as you would dahlias. Needs support.

Lilium Golden Splendor Group

1.5m (5ft)
Climate zones 3–9

Description
These are golden yellow trumpet lilies. If they're happy, they get huge. Wonderful scent. Similar, equally reliable variety in clear yellow with a crimson back to the petals is *L. regale* 'Royal Gold'. Flowers late June/July.

Role
One of the best for arranging one stem on its own in a tall, thin, glass vase or decanter.

Good combinations
I have a tall, thin, purple chemist's jar I found at an antiques market and it looks wonderful in this.

Special growing requirements
This comes back better and better each year even in partial shade in my garden. If you cut a tall stem of any of these lilies with lots of heavy heads, it tends to bend and break under the weight of the flowers. Support the bottom two thirds of the stem with a narrow cane attached with wire to its side. If you can see the cane in the vase, disguise it with green buttonhole tape, available at any florist's supply shop. Needs staking.

Lilium 'Casa Blanca'

90cm (3ft)
Climate zones 3–8

Description
An Oriental hybrid that is one of the most spectacular of the lot. It has huge, balloon-shaped flowers in pure white, with crimson stamens at the center of the flower. Fantastic fragrance. The August flowering. Pink Perfection Group is a deep, dusky crimson-pink variation on the same theme, but with trumpet-shaped flowers.

Role
This is the classic party or wedding lily. Arrange it on its own or with a bit of simple foliage.

Good combinations
Find some twisted, lichened branches or turning autumn leaves and mix them in with these, or cut some tall, straight stems of *Eucalyptus gunnii*. The lilies look beautiful showing up against the silver leaves.

Special growing requirements
If you garden on a heavy soil, avoid these spectacular Oriental hybrids. If you're lucky, they'll flower once, but probably not again. They do much better in pots and on a freely drained soil. Remove pollen-laden anthers as they ripen. Needs staking.

Lilium 'Côte d'Azur'

60cm (2ft)
Climate zones 3–9

Description
A short-stemmed lily in a deep, rich pink with a dark crimson wash over the stems. This is ideal for pots and gardens in exposed sites as it won't flop about even without a stake. Sadly, no scent.

Role
A small lily for tied bunches and moderate-sized vases. Many lilies are too big for anything but vast, show-stopping arrangements. They drown everything else, but not this one. It is just the right size.

Good combinations
Mix it with *Gladiolus communis*, eremurus, allium seed heads and euphorbia for a great midsummer bunch (see page 103).

Special growing requirements
Easy and reliable lily that will reappear for year after year. Remove pollen-laden anthers as they ripen. Needs staking.

Lilium 'Fire King'

1.2m (4ft)
Climate zones 3–9

Description
This is a less red-orange Asiatic lily than 'Gran Paradiso'. It looks good for over a month in my garden and the clump gets bigger every year. Sadly, no scent.

Role
A wonderful lily for hanging globes. It's large and dramatic enough to be seen from afar.

Good combinations
A perfect foil to crimson, or purple and acid-green.

Special growing requirements
Easy and reliable lily that will reappear for year after year. Remove pollen-laden anthers as they ripen. Needs staking.

Lilium 'Gran Paradiso'

1.2m (4ft)
Climate zones 3–9

Description
A lovely burnt orange, Asiatic hybrid. I have it planted with *Euphorbia sikkimensis*. The euphorbia has a wash of red on its stems picking up on the color of the lily. They are both at their best at the same time. Sadly, no scent.

Role
A lily in my favorite color. I pick these, one flower on its own, for putting in front of me on my desk.

Good combinations
For a perfect color contrast, place one flower in a turquoise bowl or vase (see page 98). It's also lovely with purple.

Special growing requirements
Asiatic hybrids are the so-called summer tulips, because they are so easy to grow. You only have to get them in the ground and they will flower. Every year their clump doubles in size. Remove pollen-laden anthers as they ripen. Needs staking.

Lilium 'Green Magic'

90cm (3ft)
Climate zones 3–9

Description
This is another trumpet lily with yellow centers to the flowers, brushed with green on the outside. Highly scented. Flowers late June/July.

Role
Lovely on its own, or in a spectacular mixed vase of flowers.

Good combinations
Use it floating with other lilies, or cut a few stems with a crimson-flowered lily like the Pink Perfection Group.

Special growing requirements
Grow these as for other lilies. Remove pollen-laden anthers as they ripen. Needs staking.

Lilium regale 'Album', Regal lily

90cm (3ft)
Climate zones 3–9

Description
This fragrant lily has pure white petals around a bright gold center. As with all regal lilies it will flower well for the first year and for many years after that.

Role
Arrange on its own – you don't need anything else. They will last nearly two weeks if you remove the lower flowers as they go over.

Good combinations
Pick single flower heads. The plants will still look good in the garden and you'll have flowers and fragrance in the house too.

Special growing requirements
Grow them in full sun, with good drainage. With all lilies, you need to beware of the bright scarlet lily beetle. The adult and larvae munch through bulbs, leaves and flowers. Squash them hard under foot as soon as you see them.

Lilium regale, Regal lily

90cm (3ft)
Climate zones 3–9

Description
These are beautiful and fragrant lilies. They are white, brushed with crimson on the outside. They'll be out in early June.

Role
I love these arranged on their own. If you have enough of them, pick five or seven stems and put them at the center of a large table.

Good combinations
I can't bear to pick a whole stem of lilies unless I have huge groups of them in flower. Instead, pick single flower heads from the stem, cutting one from each. Float them with other similar lilies like 'Green Magic' in a huge, shallow bowl (see page 101).

Special growing requirements
These are some of the most reliable and perennial lilies you can grow. Plant them in full sun, with good drainage. Remove pollen-laden anthers as they ripen. The pollen marks clothes and leaving them on ages the flower. Needs staking.

Nectaroscordum siculum subsp. *bulgaricum*
90cm (3ft)
Climate zones 4–10

Description
Elegant green, pink and crimson-brown allium-type flower. It looks like a candelabrum with a circle of hanging bells from the top of every stem. Flowers in July.

Role
This is a good upper story for midsummer flowers.

Good combinations
Works best with fresh colors – whites, creams and greens.

Special growing requirements
Cheap, easy to grow bulb, which will self-sow a little. It doesn't become an invasive nightmare as many of the smaller-flowered alliums do. Change the water regularly. It gets an oniony smell after three or four days, but the flowers will go on looking good for ten.

All these bulbs look spectacular arranged several stems on their own, but are even better as a magnificent bunch in a large-scale vase.

dahlias

❁ Lots of people hate dahlias. They think of them as over-complicated, formal flowers, with huge blooms, too many rows of petals, and colors too gaudy to be allowed into the garden. There are some hideous dahlias, there's no question about that, but there are some wonderful ones too, and they make superb cut flowers. ❁

Why grow dahlias?

Dahlias are frost-tender tubers, with fleshy root structures that look like a bunch of salamis on a string. If you plant them out before the frosts are over, the leaves will die.

Like annuals and biennials, dahlias are cut-and-come-again flowers. I once spent a summer working in Christopher Lloyd's garden, Great Dixter, as a volunteer. My main job was dead-heading dahlias. If you let them run to seed, they stop flowering. I filled hours removing spent flowers. But why not pick them alive, when they're looking wonderful, to take into the house? It has the same effect as dead-heading. You'll have slightly fewer flowers on show in the garden, but lots in the house.

If you keep picking them, they'll flower prolifically through the summer and most of the autumn – here in the south of England, I'm still picking dahlias in mid-November. Everyone else's gardens and cutting patches are brown and gray but, if you've got dahlias, you'll have a riot of color outside and on your kitchen table, when there's almost nothing else around.

So get to know the good ones and plant lots of them. The dark, rich colors, the deep reds, purples and near-blacks should predominate. They have a velvety glamour, which provide a bass note in the garden. Sprinkled above them, you need a few bright pinks, pink-purples and oranges for a splash of color; the top notes, like a squeeze of lemon with smoked salmon. It's good to have one or two whites and paler pinks to introduce a little calm, but don't mix these two groups together. You can combine the very dark, such as 'Alltami Corsair', 'Arabian Night' or 'Rip City', with white ones, like 'White Star', but, on the whole, the calm and the strong are best kept well apart. The whites can make the strong look heavy, even tacky – and the strong can make the pale ones bland. Each is better alone.

(Opposite) An arrangement of dahlias in colored bottles.

(Overleaf) The dahlia garden at its peak in late summer.

Making arrangements

Dahlias have a reputation for not lasting in water. It's true that some flop within a couple of days if picked with a long stem. One of my favorite dahlias, the cactus-flowered, rich purple 'Hillcrest Royal', lasts less than a day in water if picked with a stem, and the wonderful bright pink, single-flowered border cultivar, 'Fascination', is also short-lived once cut. But both will last a week, if cut with only 2.5cm (1in) of stem, and floated in water in a shallow bowl. The rest will give you four or five days, whatever the length of stem.

The only thing to remember is that buds should not be picked before they show color. Tight, green buds won't open in a vase. Use the small, dark-flowered ones, such as the decorative 'Black Fire', or the collerette, 'Inglebrook Jill', in mixed bunches with crimson antirrhinums, the orange Mexican sunflowers (*Tithonia rotundifolia*) and green tassel flower (*Amaranthus caudatus* 'Viridis'), which flower at the same time (see pages 94 and 97).

But don't just pick them for a vase. The bold, chunky heads of dahlias floating in a large, shallow bowl make marvellous table centers (see page 117). Use them like water lilies with an extra punch. You don't need to arrange them, just drop them in, with a few night-lights scattered in between.

Dahlias also look good when cut with a short stem and poked into a series of different colored glasses. With the low light of autumn, the vase colors radiate like stained glass. Contrast this with a punchy dahlia exploding out the top. Combine a deep blue bottle with an orange dahlia, such as the semi-cactus, 'Kenora Sunset'; a bright-green glass with the crimson-black of the decorative, 'Arabian Night'; a turquoise goblet with the brilliant pink of 'Geerlings Jubilee', a cactus type. Place the glasses in a line down the center of the table, or collect them together, different colors, heights and shapes in a group.

How to grow dahlias

If you're new to dahlia growing, you can buy dry tubers from a garden center, or a mail order specialist. Some specialist nurseries also offer them as rooted stem cuttings, or you can take your own stem cuttings from tubers grown on under cover (see pages 120–21). Dahlias are fast growing, so you'll get good-sized plants in one growing season from cuttings.

Starting dahlias from dry tubers

Pot the tubers up in early April, in a generous pot, at least 2 liter (3½ pint). Plant the tuber stem end upwards, 2.5–5cm (1–2in) deep, using multipurpose potting compost, and place them in a light, frost-free place, such as a cold frame or greenhouse. Keep the compost moist. They will have formed bushy plants by the time the frosts have ended and will be in flower in early July.

If you don't have a suitable place to grow the potted tubers, put them straight into the ground when the frosts are nearly over and, if the foliage appears before the frosts are over, mulch them or protect them with a cloche. This system involves less work, but you'll have plants that are several weeks behind those brought on inside.

Planting dahlias

When you plant them, be brave. Don't line them up on their own in a dahlia bed; mix them up with other plants to balance their drama. Group together three of each type and surround the group with flowering or foliage plants of contrasting color, arranging them as you might in a vase. Go for equally powerful flowers, sunflowers and tall half-hardy annuals, such as cleomes, *Verbena bonariensis* and *Tithonia*. Break up the flowers with bold foliage; use spiky and architectural leaves, such as those of the castor oil plant (*Ricinus communis*), amaranthus, phormiums, *Melianthus major*, cannas, and the large-leaved, wild tobacco plant (*Nicotiana sylvestris*).

You'll create a Rousseauesque paradise, flowering continuously until the first frosts and producing buckets of flowers for up to five months without cease.

Five keys to success with dahlias

1 Start them off under cover in a light, frost-free place. If you give them some warmth, by placing them in a propagator, or on a heated bench, they'll grow at twice the pace.

2 Pinch out the tips and remove small, spindly shoots to encourage strong growth and lots of flowers.

3 Plant them with lots of organic material at their roots and feed and water them generously.

4 Stake them securely.

5 If you live in an area with mild winters, don't dig your tubers up, mulch them deeply with 8–10cm (3–4in) of compost or straw as a blanket to protect them through the winter.

How to plant dahlias

Dahlias thrive in most sunny situations, but do best in a fertile soil, with plentiful moisture and good drainage.

Dig a hole, 30cm (12in) wide and deep, for each one, spacing them 60–90cm (2–3ft) feet apart. The larger varieties need at least 90cm (3ft) spacings, or they will crowd each other out.

You will need a stout stake, not just a bamboo cane, to support each plant and it is a good idea to knock this in first and place the plant by its side once the stake is in position. It needs to be about 30cm (1ft) shorter than the expected height of the plant.

Put the plant in the hole, and backfill with soil mixed with lots of compost or well-rotted manure, and give it a good dousing with a full watering can.

Stem thinning and pinching out

Whether you have raised your dahlias outside in the garden, or under cover, you need to remove all but five shoots sprouting from the tuber (stem thinning) with a

(Inset) Dahlia 'Jescot Julie'
(Below) Arrangement of
dahlias in a bowl (see p144).

(Page 119) Cactus dahlia
'Geerlings Jubilee' with waterlily dahlia 'Autumn Lustre'.

sharp knife. If you want to build up your stock, these can be used for stem cuttings. Then pinch out the tips of the remaining main shoots between your thumb and forefinger as they grow. Thinning and pinching out encourages bushy plants with strong, vigorous shoots that produce lots of flowers.

Feeding and watering

After about a week in the ground, scatter fish, blood, and bone fertilizer around the clump at the manufacturer's recommended rate, and give them another good soaking. From midsummer onwards, feed them every week with a liquid fertilizer that is high in nitrogen and potash, and water them at least once a week if it's dry, with a flood, not a sprinkle, for each plant. This also helps prevent powdery mildew, which can be a problem in a dry summer.

Staking

Having put the stake in place at planting, tie the shoots in every couple of weeks, as they will grow very quickly once they get going. It is really worth mastering the clove hitch knot to prevent the stem chafing against the stake (see page 51).

Dead-heading

If you don't pick every flower, try to have an occasional blitz of dead-heading. This will make them look much better and will prolong flowering. Cut spent flowerheads off by removing the whole flowering stem, back down to a fat, healthy bud.

Pests

Earwigs can be a problem with dahlias, eating the flowers and the leaves. The organic method of control is to position pots filled with straw upside-down on canes dotted throughout your dahlias. The earwigs crawl into the straw in the day. You empty the whole thing somewhere else in the garden every couple of days and let them crawl out.

Lifting and storing

In recent years, winters in the south of England have been so mild that dahlias left in the ground, mulched deeply to protect them from the frost, have survived, bulking up and flowering well before other plants grown on in pots. Even the wet autumns and winters did not kill my dahlias left in the ground. You could opt for this low-maintenance regime, but you do risk losing your plants if your winter climate brings savage frosts.

To conserve your plants for next year, after the tops have been frosted and blackened in autumn, cut the stems down to 15cm (6in) above ground level. Dig them up and knock off surplus soil. With a small stick, carefully scoop out the loose soil between the tubers – but leave enough to hold them in place. Do not clean the tubers under a tap. To get water on the tubers at this time of year spells disaster; they'll go moldy in storage if they are damp or damaged.

Label every one with its name; I use a luggage label tied on to the central stem for this. Let them dry for a couple of weeks, hanging them upside down from a dried stalk. Dust the dry tubers with yellow sulphur to discourage mold and mildew and pack them away in a storage box in peat or dry sand. This prevents the tubers from becoming desiccated. Store them in a cool, frost-free place.

Propagating dahlias

There are three main ways of building up your stock of dahlias, from stem cuttings, or by dividing the tubers. I love the species from which many of the cultivars have been bred, and these are easily grown from seed. Sow them as you would half-hardy annuals, under cover in early April (see page 88). Look out for *Dahlia merckii*, with flowers in bright lilac-pink, and the red *D. coccinea*. Sadly, both last only two or three days once cut.

(Below) Late summer color with *Dahlia* 'Alltami Corsair' **and *Amaranthus* 'Intense Purple' in the foreground.**

Dividing tubers

When you bring your dahlias out of their winter store in early spring, you can divide large and healthy tubers into sections to make more plants. To be viable, each part must have a piece of stem with a complete tuber, so don't chop one of the hanging salamis in half. Pot each section into multipurpose compost. Some people do this in the autumn, but it's safest done in the spring, when you can cut out any rot that developed while in store before you pot them up.

How to take stem cuttings

If you want to multiply your dahlias by this method, pot up the tubers by late spring (February or early March) – a few weeks earlier than usual. You'll then have shoots long enough for cuttings by the middle of April, which will be well-rooted, and ready for putting out in the garden by the time the frosts finish.

1 When the shoots are 5–7cm (2–3in) long, with 2–3 pairs of leaves and a growing point, take the cuttings. Cut each stem with a sharp knife at right angles, taking it close to the base.

2 Remove the tip and trim the stem just above a leaf joint to leave one pair of leaves, discarding the rest.

3 Cut the remaining pair of leaves in half to reduce their surface area. (Left whole, they will dry the cutting out and make it flop, and flopping prevents rooting and/or encourages rot.)

4 Push the cuttings into a moist and gritty multipurpose compost. Arrange four or five of them around the edge of a 10cm (4in) pot. I don't use hormone rooting powder as cuttings root easily without it. Water the cuttings carefully.

5 Keep the cuttings moist at all times. This is easiest if they are enclosed, so make your own polythene bag tent with canes. Cut a green, or bamboo cane into 30cm (12in) sections and poke three or four into the compost, around the outer edge of the pot. Put a large polythene bag over the canes and secure it with a rubber band about a third of the way up the pot's side. This keeps all the moisture in and prevents the cuttings from collapsing. The canes hold the plastic away from the dahlia leaves; if they touch it, rot may set in.

6 Place the pot in a warm, light place, preferably in a heated propagator, if you have one. Turn the bags daily to stop excess condensation building up, which can encourage rot. With warmth at the base, they will root in three to four weeks.

7 Take them out of their pot, tease the roots apart and pot them up individually. Grow them on for another couple of weeks in a light, frost-free place, keeping the compost moist.

8 When the plants have formed four pairs of leaves, nip out the tip just above the third pair. This will encourage the growth of bushy plants. They're now ready to put out in the garden, if frosts are over. Harden them off by exposing them gradually to cooler conditions before you plant them out.

Dahlias to grow

Dahlias are grouped according to the structure of their flower. Many of the groups have small-, medium- and large-flowered cultivars. The large-flowered ones are bred mainly for exhibition and tend to look over-the-top in the garden, with flowers the size of hats. Grow one or two of the giants – they look funny in the garden if you only have a few, and marvellous floating in a bowl of water at the center of a table, but concentrate mainly on the small- and medium-sized flowers. The only groups that I don't like are ball dahlias – fully double, globular flowers – and pompons, which are similar to ball dahlias, but smaller. They look like the things cheerleaders wave around in the air – too girly, perfect and uptight for me. **In climate zones 4–7, dahlias may be planted in containers and harvested in autumn. In warmer zones, mulch dahlias for winter protection.**

(Opposite)
***Dahlia* 'Jescot Julie'**

'Alstergruss'
Collerette

60cm (2ft)

Description
Superb orange dahlia with a clear brightness. Compact plants, ideal for containers and the front of a border.

Role
Use in small vases, or floating in a shallow bowl (see page 117).

Good combinations
Wonderful color to contrast with bright pink, crimson and purple. Float it in a turquoise bowl.

'Arabian Night'
Decorative

90cm (3ft)

Description
Old-fashioned cultivar with medium-sized flowers in velvety crimson-black.

Role
Wonderful as a single stem.

Good combinations
Arrange on its own, or with orange, gold and acid-green.

'Bishop of Llandaff'
Border

90cm (3ft)

Description
Brilliant velvety scarlet flowers with elegant, finely cut crimson foliage. The best foliage of all dahlias.

Role
Very bright for using in mixed bunches. Best as a single stem, or floated in a bowl.

Good combinations
Arrange with lots of other bright dahlias, floating in a bowl.

'Fascination'
Border

60cm (2ft)

Description
Crimson foliage with bright, cerise-pink flowers, with three rows of petals around a golden center.

Role
Won't last on a long stem. Best picked and floated in a bowl.

Good combinations
Float it in a turquoise or acid-green bowl. Wonderful growing in pots.

'Gerrie Hoek'
Waterlily

1.2m (4ft)

Description
Pale, silvery pink with wiry stems; excellent for cutting.

Role
Float in a shallow bowl, or pick for large arrangements.

Good combinations
Lovely mixed with other pinks and whites.

'Alltami Corsair'
Semi-cactus

1.2m (4ft)

Description
Elegant, wine-red flowers, the color and shape of a sea anemone on steroids!

Role
For large vases, or floating bowls.

Good combinations
Wonderful in a bowl of floating dahlias of every different color you have.

'Autumn Lustre'
Waterlily

1.2m (4ft)

Description
Good bronze-orange, rather than tangerine, with small flowers on strong and very productive plants.

Role
Ideal for hand-tied and mixed vases.

Good combinations
Lovely with the deep purples and crimson-blacks.

'Black Fire'
Decorative

90cm (3ft)

Description
Prolific flowerer in deepest dark crimson.

Role
It has small, neat flowers, which are ideal for picking and using in mixed bunches.

Good combinations
Arrange with orange and other crimsons.

'Geerlings Jubilee'
Cactus

1.2m (4ft)

Description
One of the spikiest. Large, spectacular, show-stopping pink.

Role
For vases or bowls.

Good combinations
Perfect with spiky 'White Star' in a blue bowl or vase. I also love this with turquoise-blue hydrangeas.

'Hillcrest Royal'
Cactus

1.2m (4ft)

Description
Very productive plants with the spikiest flowers in bright magenta-purple.

Role
Won't last on a long stem, so pick for floating.

Good combinations
Float with lots of other dahlias in a color razzmatazz.

'Jescot Julie'
Orchid-flowered

90cm (3ft)

Description
Orange petals with a
purple-crimson
reverse to each one.
Unusual and elegant.

Role
Use in any
arrangement – a tied
bunch, vase, single
stem, or floating in a
shallow bowl.

Good combinations
Arrange with crimson
or purple.

'Raffles'
Decorative

90cm (3ft)

Description
Orange, washed pink
dahlia with neat
flowers, the perfect
size for smaller
bunches.

Role
Wonderful in a tied
bunch with pink
cleomes and green
Nicotiana alata.

Good combinations
Very long-lasting as a
cut flower.

'Rip City'
Semi-cactus

90cm (3ft)

Description
The darkest dahlia I
know – the color of
beetroot juice running
over a white plate.
Large flowers.

Role
For globes, large
vases or bowls (see
page 137).

Good combinations
My favorite dahlia of
all, wonderful with
white and orange.

'Inglebrook Jill'
Collerette

1.2m (4ft)

Description
Velvet, plum-crimson
petals around a golden
center. Lovely and rich.

Role
Use in small vases,
or floating in a
shallow bowl.

Good combinations
Float in a turquoise
bowl with the bright
orange collerette
'Alstergruss'.

'Kenora Sunset'
Semi-cactus

1.2m (4ft)

Description
Yellow, tipped red-
orange flowers, as
bright and gaudy as
they come.

Role
For globes, large
vases, or bowls (see
page 137).

Good combinations
Superb as a splash
amongst lots of rich,
dark chocolatey
dahlias.

'Requiem'
Decorative

90cm (3ft)

Description
Lovely bright pink-
purple flowers, the
size of my palm.

Role
Use a single stem,
or float in a shallow
bowl.

Good combinations
Arrange with orange,
and also with crimson
and acid-green.